ZAYN

A NEW DIRECTION

THE UNAUTHORIZED BIOGRAPHY

SARAH OLIVER

LESSER
GODS

FIRST PUBLISHED IN THE UNITED STATES OF AMERICA IN 2016 BY:
Lesser Gods, 15 W. 36th St., 8th Fl., New York, NY 10018,
an imprint of Overamstel Publishers, Inc.
PHONE (646) 850-4201
www.lessergodsbooks.com

Originally published in the United Kingdom by
John Blake Publishing Ltd in 2015

DISTRIBUTED BY: Consortium Book Sales & Distribution
34 13th Ave. NE #101, Minneapolis, MN 55413
PHONE (800) 283-3572 www.cbsd.com

FIRST U.S. UPDATED EDITION September 2016 / 10 9 8 7 6 5 4 3 2 1
PRINTED AND BOUND IN THE U.S.A.

ISBN: 978-1-944713-08-9
LIBRARY OF CONGRESS CONTROL NUMBER: 2016939180

Dedicated, with love, to the children of Spinney Avenue and Rainford Brook Lodge Primary Schools.

CONTENTS

CHAPTER ONE

1993: A STAR IS BORN

Zayn Malik is from East Bowling in Bradford and he was born on January 12, 1993 at St. Luke's Hospital, Bradford. His parents, Yaser and Trisha Malik, were so excited when he was born—he was their first son and a great playmate for little Doniya, who was one at the time. Zayn's wider family was really happy, too.

In Arabic, the name Zayn means "beautiful" and Malik, his surname, means "king" or "chieftain." Yaser and Trisha gave him the middle name Javadd, which means "generous" in Arabic. They spelled his first name "Zain" and when Zayn was on *The X Factor* he was referred to as "Zain" but he prefers it to be spelled "Zayn," so after the show he made sure that he would be known as Zayn from then on.

When Zayn was growing up he was always full of energy. He loved being the center of attention and he liked to sing and dance. His parents had two more children after Zayn: Waliyha and Safaa. Waliyha is six years younger and Safaa is ten years Zayn's junior, but the family are all still very close. Zayn has said the one thing that's guaranteed to make him smile is talking to his little sister Safaa.

Zayn would put on shows for his parents and as he grew up, he kept on performing for them, along with his sisters. He would do his own versions of Daniel Bedingfield tracks like "If You're Not The One" and dreamt of performing onstage. His mom admitted to the *Mirror* in April 2012: "I have quite a few videos of him singing as a little boy but he's banned me from showing anyone. My favorite is him singing "I Believe I Can Fly" [by R. Kelly], wearing a green [bathrobe]."

Zayn is close to his dad, who looked after him before he went to school. He was very hyperactive so Yaser had his hands full! Both Zayn and his dad love drawing and art. In fact when 1D were being interviewed for *You Generation* in March 2013, Zayn was challenged to draw a picture of his favorite member of the band in one minute. He chose Louis and the sketch he did was really good. In the same interview Niall did a brilliant impression of Zayn. The interview is available on YouTube.

Growing up, Zayn loved spending time with his family's pets, and he still is a huge animal lover. They had two cats called Lily and Lolo and a Staffordshire bull terrier called

Tyson. The Malik family now have two cats called Rolo and Tom and a dog named Boris.

Even though Zayn didn't go to preschool he was still really excited about starting elementary school. He liked playing in the sand with the other children and listening to his teacher read stories to the class. Though small for his age, he was very intelligent. By the time he was ten years old he could read difficult books that even teenagers might have struggled with. Back home, he practiced reading a lot with his grandfather, who encouraged him to push himself.

But school wasn't always a happy place for Zayn. Often he felt like the odd one out because there were no other children like him. No one else was of mixed heritage (Zayn's dad is British Pakistani and his mom is half Irish and half English) and the other children would ask him why his dad was brown and his mom was white. This made him feel pretty isolated, but thankfully he had his sisters to turn to. Zayn only stayed at his first elementary school for two years before moving to another one, where he was much happier. He met his best friend Sam at Lower Fields Primary School and they had lots of fun together until they moved schools and drifted apart.

At elementary and then later in high school Zayn's nickname was "Z" (pronounced "Zed").

Zayn ended up going to lots of different educational establishments, for a whole host of different reasons. He admitted to *Sugar* magazine in March 2013: "I got expelled from a couple of schools for fighting.

"Where I'm from, you kind of had to get into a couple of scrapes to survive."

While at Tong High School, Zayn was caught with a BB gun and got into lots of trouble. He hadn't fired it at anyone but that didn't matter, his teachers still had to punish him for having an imitation firearm. Whenever he started at a new school he would get lots of attention from girls, who wanted to know everything about him because he was new, which made Zayn feel cool. He liked getting extra attention.

Zayn has always loved singing and one of his earliest gigs was while he was a student at Lower Fields Primary School and he sang in a choir for the Lord Mayor at his local supermarket. At Tong High School Zayn combined singing with acting when he played the lead in their production of *Bugsy Malone*. He didn't get nervous, although he sang in front of four hundred people in the audience. Zayn also appeared in the school's production of *The Arabian Nights* and had a part created for him in the musical *Grease*. He wasn't old enough to be a T-Bird so his teacher created a young T-Bird part for him and one for his friend, Aqib Khan.

Today, Aqib Khan is a professional actor and he played Sajid Khan in the 2010 film *West Is West* and Rashid Jarwar in the ITV series *The Jury II*. If you search on YouTube, you can see a short clip of Zayn and Aqib in *Grease*—they both look really young.

At Tong High, acting was Zayn's real passion and singing was his second love. His three favorite subjects at school were English, art and drama. In fact, Zayn was so good at English that he sat his English GCSE (General Certificate of Secondary Education Exam) a year early. Steve Gates, assistant head teacher, told the *Telegraph & Argus*: "Zayn is a model student who excelled in all the performing arts subjects, one of the specialist subjects here at Tong.

"He was always a star performer in all the school productions so it was no surprise when Simon Cowell threw him his big chance."

He joined the school choir at the request of another teacher, Mrs. Fox, who thought he had a good voice. Around this time he became best friends with a boy called Danny, who was in his drama class and also befriended Danny's younger brother, Anthony. Today, they are still close and chill out whenever Zayn is visiting Bradford. They love playing on Xbox together and share the same sense of humor. If you google "Zayn Malik, Anthony Riach & Danny Riach Dancing" you will see a great video of the three of them dancing to an Usher song—and they can seriously dance!

One day, when Zayn was at school, he was given the opportunity to sing with British singer-songwriter/rapper Jay Sean. Jay remembers the day well and explained to 2DAY FM in June 2012: "About five years ago I happened to be at a school in England and I was doing, like, these talks about music and who wants to be a musician and blah, blah, blah. So anyway, I was on stage singing and then I went out to the crowd and I was like, 'Are there any aspiring singers over here?' and then this little boy puts his hand up and I was like, 'You, come up here, man!' and I was like, 'Have you ever sung before?' and he was like, 'No, I'm really shy, I'm really nervous,' and I was like, 'Listen, we're going to do this together. We're going to sing one of my songs and we're going to do it together, me and you.' "

Jay Sean and Zayn sang the song "Ride It" and the experience was to leave a lasting impression on Zayn. It was the first time he had sung on stage and it really boosted his confidence. After Zayn found fame with 1D he tweeted Jay Sean to ask him if he remembered that day, and to say a big thank you.

In the summer before starting at sixth-form college (the equivalent of 11th and 12th grade in the US), Zayn grew a lot so he was no longer small for his age. Some of his classmates were really shocked when they saw him that September—he looked like a new person; he had grown so much. He had started boxing in his spare time and later confessed to the *Daily Star* in April 2013: "I did boxing from when I was fifteen to seventeen. I love it and I've started training again now on the side, even though we don't get much time off for exercise.

"I'm trying to eat healthier so I can bulk up. I'd love to pursue it properly one day."

CHAPTER TWO

TIME TO SHINE

Zayn would never have auditioned for *The X Factor* if it hadn't been for his music teacher, who told him to go for it. For two years he had the application form but never sent it in—he was just too nervous. Zayn auditioned in Manchester on July 27, 2010 and was given the number 165616 when he registered (Louis's audition number was 155204, Liam's was 61898, Niall's was 232677 and Harry's number was 165998). He nearly backed out but his mom encouraged him, with Zayn later admitting to the *Telegraph & Argus* newspaper: "I was really nervous but she told me just to get on with it and not miss my chance." If it wasn't for Trisha, Zayn could have missed out on the opportunity to be in One Direction.

The first people that Zayn had to impress were not the judges but the backstage production team. They judge everyone before choosing their favorites to return on a second day to sing for Simon Cowell, Nicole Scherzinger and Louis Walsh. Thousands of people wanted to get through so Zayn had his work cut out to impress them. The production team only pick the very best (and the absolute worst) singers to make it through to the next round. Zayn was over the moon when he was told that he was good enough, and his family was very proud. All he had to do now was make sure his nerves didn't get the best of him.

Zayn chose to sing "Let Me Love You" by Mario. He decided to dress casually for his audition rather than wear something too dressy. Backstage, his proud mom, dad and sister waited with host Dermot O'Leary and they clapped every time they heard a judge say, "Yes." Zayn got a "yes" from all three judges so he knew he was going through to *X Factor* Bootcamp!

It was really disappointing for Zayn's family and friends that his audition was left out from *The X Factor* and *The Xtra Factor* audition shows when they aired on television. Only Harry and Liam's auditions made *The X Factor* audition shows and Niall's performance was shown on *The Xtra Factor*. Louis also missed out. At this stage *The X Factor* producers must have thought that Zayn and Louis were not going to make the live shows and so they decided to showcase other singers instead. Poor Zayn; he had done so well in his audition and he deserved to have his performance shown at the time. However, some One Direction fans later began an online petition to get Zayn's and Louis's auditions aired on TV or put on YouTube and it worked. After the final was over, their auditions were broadcast on TV for the very first time and the fans could see how well Zayn did.

In fact, Zayn did so well standing on stage and singing for the judges in his first audition because there were thousands of people watching in the audience. He needed to impress them as well as the judges, so he had to try and mask his shyness, which improved his performance. In an interview for Vevo in 2012 he revealed: "Before *X Factor* I'd never done anything that required me to have to speak in front of cameras or in front of people. *The X Factor* kinda helped me with that because you're followed around by cameras and you get used to it."

Zayn never thought he'd make it to the finals of *The X Factor*. He entered the show "just for the experience."

For the Bootcamp stage he had to head for London, leaving his family behind. From then on, things would be even tougher because, of course, the judges had chosen only the best singers to make it through. Bootcamp was held at Wembley Arena over five days in July 2010 to whittle down the 211 acts that had survived the first round. All the singers had to be at the Arena early on July 22, because they had a lot to fit in. Zayn had to stand with the other guys—he would be in the Boys' category if he made it through. The Boys were told to practice "Man In The Mirror" by Michael Jackson. The Girls had to practice Beyoncé's "If I Were A

Boy," while the Groups practiced "Nothing's Gonna Stop Us Now" by Starship, and the Over-25s had to sing Lady Gaga's "Poker Face." At this stage none of the contestants' first auditions had been shown on TV so Zayn had no idea who the favorites in the Boys' category were.

He must have been feeling nervous when Simon Cowell told all the singers: "By the end of the day, half of you are going home. Today you're going to be put into your categories and you're going to sing one song. There are literally no second chances today."

Zayn really didn't want to end up on the train back to Bradford that night and so he had to make his version of "Man In The Mirror" really stand out from all the other hopefuls. He was under a lot of pressure, but this is what Cowell and Louis Walsh were after: they wanted to push these aspiring pop stars hard to get the best out of them. In their first auditions the singers had been able to choose any song they liked, but their first Bootcamp song was something selected for them.

Zayn did really well—his performance of "Man In The Mirror" was great and he showed the judges what a talented singer he was. Other singers failed to perform to his level and some even struggled to remember the lyrics. Harry, Liam, Louis and Niall also did well at this stage but because they were all auditioning as solo artists at this point they were competing against each other.

Zayn was thrilled when told that he was to come back for Day 2: he had made the next round and wouldn't be going home that night. He knew that Day 2 would be even tougher, though, because already so many good singers had been asked to leave. Afterward, he rang his family to let them know Day 1 had been a success; he then tried to get some sleep.

On arrival at Wembley the next day, Zayn and the remaining singers were instructed to go to the stage. Simon Cowell and Louis Walsh introduced them to Brian Friedman, international choreographer and dancer, who would be teaching them how to dance. One of the best choreographers in the world, Friedman has worked with Britney Spears, Beyoncé and Mariah Carey, among others.

He told the singers: "I don't want you to be scared. What we are going to work on is your stage presence and choreography."

There had never been a dance element at Bootcamp before so Simon Cowell and the other judges had no idea what it would be like, but they wanted to challenge the contestants to try something new. Simon reassured the singers that no one would be eliminated if their dancing skills weren't up to scratch but they still had to give 110 percent.

Zayn tried his best in rehearsals but he struggled to pick up the choreography and it made him feel like a failure. He felt he was so bad that he couldn't perform in front of Simon. When the boys were called on stage to show the judges what they had learned, Zayn stayed backstage and he must have thought that his *X Factor* dream was over. Simon, Louis and Brian Friedman watched the boys dance, picking out their favorite dancers. Before Brian could dismiss the boys and call on the next group of dancers, though, Simon asked him where Zayn was—he had noticed that he was missing. At first Brian didn't know but after asking around, he discovered that Zayn was backstage, refusing to come out. Simon decided that they couldn't go on without Zayn so he personally went backstage to request him to dance.

Zayn told the backstage camera: "I seriously don't want to do it because I hate dancing and I've never done it before, and I feel like an idiot on the stage with other people who are clearly better than me and I just feel like an idiot—I'm not doing it.

"I just know I'm going to do it wrong because I don't know it. When you've got to perform in front of Simon and professionals that know what they're doing and how to dance, and professional choreographers and stuff, and I just don't know . . ."

Usually Simon Cowell would have had no time for someone who refused to do what he wanted him to do but he felt that he had to help Zayn. He had been so impressed by the young man's singing the day before and didn't want him to make the biggest mistake ever and leave because of his reluctance to dance. It was the kind of decision that Zayn could end up regretting for the rest of his life.

Simon asked him: "Zayn, why aren't you out there? Why aren't you out there? You can't just bottle it . . . you can't just hide behind here. Zayn, you are ruining this for yourself! I'm trying to help you here. So, if you can't do it now, you'll [sic] never gonna be able to do it, right? Come on, let's go and do it."

Zayn couldn't ignore Simon's advice and so he decided to give it a go. Just before he went on stage, Simon told him: "Don't do that again, get on with it." They quickly shook hands and Simon went back to his position next to Louis and Brian.

Simon allowed Harry and a few of the other boys to dance again with Zayn so that he wouldn't have to do it on his own. Zayn wasn't great but he wasn't that bad either and although Simon thought he looked "uncomfortable," he was impressed that Zayn had tried. Afterward, the reluctant dancer must have been relieved that it was all over and he told the cameras that he would now work on his dance skills and his confidence levels.

On the third day of Bootcamp, Zayn and the other contestants met the third judge, former Pussycat Dolls' singer Nicole Scherzinger. She had been impressed with Zayn after his first audition, but he knew that he must impress her again if he was to make the "Judges' Houses" round. Nicole was a surprise addition to the show because the third Bootcamp judge was supposed to be former Girls Aloud singer Cheryl Cole, but she was recovering from malaria. (She had contracted the disease after climbing Mount Kilimanjaro to raise money for charity.) Nicole would simply be taking Cheryl's place at Bootcamp and then at the Judges' Houses stage, but Cheryl would hopefully be back soon.

Because of the changes to the judges' line-up, *The X Factor* producers chose to cancel the live element of Bootcamp. They tweeted: "Due to the unusual circumstances, we are not inviting an audience to watch the contestants perform at *The X Factor* boot camp." Although this announcement disappointed thousands of people who had been looking forward to catching a first glimpse of the contestants it must have helped the Bootcamp residents, who were no doubt feeling nervous and lacking in confidence. Zayn could simply concentrate on impressing Simon, Louis and Nicole—the three judges who had given him three "yeses" in the first audition round—rather than think of the thousands of people watching in the arena.

For their final performances the singers were given a list of forty songs and told to find one number to sing that would showcase their voice. No one could afford to pick the wrong song but they couldn't make too safe a choice either because they were required to perform it in a different slant, treating it in their own unique way. Zayn chose "Make You Feel My Love" by Bob Dylan, which incidentally is the exact same song that Louis chose to sing!

After Zayn had performed it must have been hard as he made his way backstage because the judges didn't give him any feedback at all—they just said "thanks" and there was no hint of what they thought in their facial expressions. All Zayn and the other contestants could do was go back to the hotel and try to sleep. The next day the judges would decide who would be going through to Judges' Houses, so he wannabe pop stars had an anxious wait ahead.

It might have been tough on Zayn and the other singers but the fifth and final day of Bootcamp was tough on the judges too, because there had been so many talented singers that it really was hard to pick just six in each category to make it through. In the end they decided to choose eight singers for each category and to slightly adjust the older category so that it was Over-28s instead of Over-25s.

There were thirty talented boys left in the competition so the atmosphere was tense when they were called onto the stage to learn their fate. As the judges started calling out the names of the singers who had made it through, Zayn was incredibly nervous.

Simon was the first to speak, saying: "The first person through to the Judges' Houses is . . . John Wilding."

Nicole: "Nicolo Festa."

Louis: "Paije Richardson."

Simon: "Aiden Grimshaw."

Louis: "Marlon McKenzie."

Louis: "Karl Brown."

Nicole: "Matt Cardle."

Simon Cowell: "The final contestant who's made it through is Tom Richards . . . That's it, guys, I'm really sorry."

To get so close and then to be rejected was really hard for Zayn to take—he had wanted so much to perform on The *X Factor* stage. Of course the other singers who failed to get through were equally gutted. Liam, Niall and Harry were so upset that they were crying. In fact, Liam told host Dermot O'Leary: "I just don't want to go home, I just don't want to go!"

Niall said that it was one of the worst things he'd ever had to do in his life—"Standing there, waiting for your name to be called, and then it's not."

All that was left for them to do was to collect their belongings before leaving the arena. But just before they could go a member of the production team came and asked Zayn, Liam, Louis, Niall and Harry to go and wait on the stage alongside four girls: Sophia Wardman, Geneva Lane, Esther Campbell and Rebecca Creighton. Zayn didn't know what was happening but he hoped they were about to be given a second chance and he was right. Nicole Scherzinger was the first to speak once they had lined up on stage, with Zayn in the middle: "Hello, thank you so much for coming back. Judging from some of your faces, this is really hard. We've thought long and hard about it and we've thought of each of you as individuals, and we just feel that you're too talented to let go of. We think it would be a great idea to have two separate groups." Simon teased that they should form groups and that they might meet again in the future, before saying: "We've decided to put you both through . . . This is a lifeline—you've got to work ten, twelve, fourteen hours a day, every single day, and take this opportunity. You've got a real shot here, guys." Up until then it was sounding like the judges wanted them to audition the following year. Zayn's dream wasn't over yet!

The boys had to have a think and decide whether they wanted to form a group but Zayn's mind was made up: he wanted to give it a go. He told American talk show host

Barbara Walters in December 2012: "It was a no-brainer—we just wanted to see how far we could get in the competition, and so we were like, 'Cool, let's give it a go.' "

Even though the boys found out in July that they had made it through to the Judges' Houses round, they were sworn to secrecy so they couldn't tell their friends. They had to keep it quiet for months as the Bootcamp episodes were not being shown on TV until Saturday October 2 and Sunday October 3, 2010.

CHAPTER THREE

IMPRESSING SIMON

The boys didn't find out who would be their judge and mentor until after Bootcamp. It could have been Louis Walsh, Dannii Minogue, Cheryl Cole or Simon Cowell, but the person they really wanted was Simon because of his experience. The boys got their wish, but that meant they really had to work hard in the weeks leading up to Judges' Houses because Simon is a really hard judge to impress.

Initially, Simon was disappointed that he was given the Groups' category, as his first choice was the Girls' category and his second choice was the Boys. He had no idea how strong Zayn, Harry, Louis, Liam and Niall were because he had yet to see them perform together.

From day one, the boys were determined that they were going to succeed and make *The X Factor* live shows. In previous series of *The X Factor* when the judges had formed groups often they had felt disappointed by the result, even though the group members had been offered a lifeline. The boys knew that the standard of groups that had made the Judges' Houses round was high, so they had to rehearse like crazy to make sure they were the best. They were eager for Simon to forget that he had just formed them when they sang; they wanted to sound like they had been singing together for years.

Just a few days after returning home from Bootcamp, Niall, Liam and Louis made their way to Harry's home in Holmes Chapel, Cheshire. His mom (Anne Cox) had offered to have them stay for a few weeks. Zayn had commitments at home so couldn't be there for the first three days but the second he could, he was there. He didn't have to catch a train or get a bus because Louis came to Bradford to pick him up in his Renault Clio. Because it was summer break, Zayn didn't have to miss school and so he could tell people at home that he was going on vacation—he couldn't reveal how far he had got in the competition.

It actually worked out well that the boys were from different parts of England (and Ireland) because it made them commit to spending twenty-four hours a day with each other at Harry's home. Had they lived locally, they might have met up only in the daytime and then gone home in the evenings, but because they were far away from where they lived, they had no alternative but to stay together. In fact, they ended up spending almost three weeks in each other's company, rehearsing and getting to know each other.

Zayn found the time intense and because he was the last to arrive, at first he felt a bit like the odd one out. However, he soon got to see the best and worst parts of his new bandmates and this ultimately helped him bond with them. During their stay, the boys rehearsed songs by Jay Sean and Jason Derulo.

The boys enjoyed themselves during their time at Harry's home but they also made sure they rehearsed, too. They had their fair share of petty squabbles but this was to be expected as they had only just met each other at Bootcamp. Because they had each entered the competition as solo artists they all had their own ideas about the type of singer they wanted to be and the kind of songs they wanted to sing. However, they knew Simon was to choose their song for Judges' Houses so the decision was out of their control. They just needed to work on their harmonies and figure out who would be the best to sing the lead vocals—not an easy decision because they were all equally talented. Each one tried out different roles, and after much discussion, they found their places in the overall group.

In the beginning Zayn's musical tastes differed to that of the others. He loved hip-hop and R&B, as he explained to *Billboard.com*: "I had kind of pigeonholed myself a little bit, so I was very aware that the guys had different musical tastes. It really broadened my taste. I listen to a lot more different stuff now, Kings of Leon, The Script. I think there's so many great bands out there I hadn't really heard before and now I get to listen to them."

As well as working, the bandmates also found time for lots of fun. Harry's mom Anne had been having some building work done on the house so there was a tractor-type machine there and the boys decided to drive it when the workmen went home, knocking things down. Zayn also managed to set fire to half a sofa, too—something Anne can't have been too happy about!

During the weeks leading up to Judges' Houses the boys had to come up with a name for their group that summed up who they were and what they were about. It was really difficult because they didn't want something that sounded foolish or had no meaning behind it. It was Harry who came up with the name One Direction quite by accident—it just popped into his head. The other boys thought it was a great name as they all wanted the same thing, and they were all going in one direction—straight to the top of the charts!

Zayn explained how the name came about to Hot 95.7FM Phoenix in June 2012. He said: "Basically we just came up with the idea to make loads of names up and it was one of the first names Harry came up with. He just texted it to us and we were like, 'Yeah, I like that, it's cool.'

"There were some really embarrassing ones that Liam came up with . . . What was the other one? USP—Unique Selling Point."

Louis added: "That is the WORST! Although to be fair, you have to be brave even to mention it in the first place. I think it came from his dad . . . Sorry, Geoff!"

For the Judges' Houses round the boys needed one unified look that would make them seem like a group, without appearing to be clones of one another. They chatted about what they might wear and eventually decided on grey or white pumps, casual shorts or three-quarter-length pants, with loose-fitting shirts or T-shirts. Zayn wore blue pants with a white T-shirt.

For Zayn, waiting in the airport for their flight to Spain felt strange because he had never been abroad before. Prior to *The X Factor* the furthest he had ever been away from home was Birmingham—and that's just eighty-eight miles away from Bradford! The boys would be competing against seven other groups in the days to come so the pressure was certainly on. Thankfully, they all had each other for support and their families were only at the other end of the phone if they needed to ask their advice or if they got homesick.

Once they landed, they were driven to their new temporary home: Simon's rented villa in Marbella. They found it hard to take in just how grand the place was—there were three swimming pools, twenty bedrooms, a movie theater and so much more. It was like nothing they had ever seen before.

While in Marbella, Zayn and Louis snuck off together even though this wasn't allowed. They got some pizza and chatted on the beach. For Zayn, it was the perfect first trip abroad!

One day, when the boys were visiting the beach, Louis was stung by a sea urchin and ended up being rushed to hospital. While concerned for their friend, the boys couldn't help but think that they might have to perform as a four-piece band. Zayn told *The X Factor* cameras: "We're all panicking a little bit 'cause we're not sure what's going to happen or when he's going to get here." Liam added: "For us that's really bad as we haven't had that much time to practice as we've only just got together as a group. I hope he's back as we really do need him."

Luckily, Louis wasn't kept in hospital and was allowed to return to Simon's villa just in time for the boys' performance. The bandmates performed "Torn," a ballad by Australian-British singer/songwriter Natalie Imbruglia. Liam sang the verse, Harry took on the chorus, Niall and Louis harmonized and Zayn finished the song perfectly. Despite their nerves it couldn't have gone any better. After finishing the song the boys had to leave the performance area and just wait to find out if they had done enough. Once they were out of earshot, Simon told his helper, American eighties singer Sinitta: "They're cool, they're relevant."

Harry summed up how the boys were feeling, telling *X Factor* cameras: "Your hunger for it grows and grows as you get through each stage in the competition. It's just the biggest stage to be told yes or no. It's one word that can change your life forever because it won't be the same if you get a "yes" and if you get a "no" then it's straight back to doing stuff that kind of drives you to come here in the first place."

One Direction's rivals and the songs they sang at Judges' Houses

Belle Amie sang "Faith" by George Michael

Diva Fever sang "Love Machine" by Girls Aloud

FYD sang "Beggin" by Madcon

Hustle sang "Tainted Love" by Soft Cell

Princes and Rogues sang "Video Killed The Radio Star"
    by The Buggles

The Reason sang "If You're Not The One"
    by Daniel Bedingfield

Twem sang "When Love Takes Over" by Kelly Rowland

One Direction hadn't been one of the groups that Simon had thought would definitely make *The X Factor* live shows but after their performance at Judges' Houses they had proved themselves to be real contenders. Other groups who Simon had believed would excel at this stage failed to make an impact, a fact that made choosing his top three really difficult.

After they were called by the production team and told to go and see Simon the boys were close to tears because they knew they were about to learn their fate and whether all the hard work they had put in had been worth it. As they lined up in front of Simon, Zayn had his arms around Liam and Louis; all five boys connected to each other for support. Simon said: "My head is saying it's a risk and my heart is saying that you deserve a shot. And that's why it's been difficult . . . So I've made a decision . . . Guys, I've gone with my heart—you're through!"

The boys shouted "Yes!" with excitement and had a massive group hug. Harry then ran over to hug Simon, closely followed by Niall and Zayn. To see their reaction, take a look on YouTube—Zayn looks so happy. Louis, Niall and Harry all had tears in their eyes—they were so overcome with emotion. Simon told the boys: "I am so impressed with all of you, I mean that."

Zayn couldn't wait to call his family and tell them the good news—for the next few months he would be singing on live TV every Saturday night!

CHAPTER FOUR

SINGING TO MILLIONS

The boys all lived at home with their families at this point but on their return to the UK, they had to get ready to move into a luxury house in London with the other *X Factor* contestants. It would be their new home for as long as they were in the competition. Zayn was excited but it was daunting to say goodbye to his family and friends in Bradford. He would only get to see them at weekends when they came to watch the live shows, and he was going to be so busy rehearsing all the time.

The boys' favorite room was the chill-out room, which had a big couch, lots of beanbags, a Ping-Pong table, huge TV and a Wii. They also liked spending time in the music room, which held a jukebox and a piano. It was pretty cramped as they had to sleep on bunk beds in a small room, but Zayn didn't mind—he was just so happy to be one step closer towards achieving his dream of landing a recording contract.

The first night Zayn and the other boys moved into the *X Factor* house all the contestants decided to have a sing-along together to celebrate being there and getting to the live shows. For the first week they could all relax because these productions hadn't yet started but once they did, the aspiring pop stars would have to be prepared to say goodbye to a solo artist or group every week. Sunday nights became difficult because the singer who'd been voted off had to come back, pack their bags and leave. Countering the sadness, Zayn and the other boys were happy to have made it through to another week, though.

During *The X Factor*, Zayn and the boys had to spend up to eighteen hours a day rehearsing to get the harmonies right and to make sure their performances were the best they could be. But they were never complacent; every week they thought they might be the ones going home. They found it was much harder being part of a group than being a solo artist because they had to all have an input and the harmonies had to be spot on. They were determined that they would share the lead singer responsibilities because all five were talented singers and they wanted to show people what each of them could do.

X FACTOR LIVE SHOWS – WEEK BY WEEK
Week 1 – Number 1s

October 9, 2010 was a monumental day for Zayn, Liam, Louis, Niall and Harry, and the other eleven acts picked at Judges' Houses. At the start of the show four wildcards were revealed, one for each judge. Simon Cowell's wildcard group were Diva Fever. Although the boys had been rehearsing for weeks, Zayn was struggling with his nerves. He was having problems coming in on time with his vocals and thought that if it happened in the live show, he would ruin things for the others. Of course none of the boys wanted to be sent home in the first week. Thankfully, on the night Zayn did come in on time and together they performed a great version of "Viva La Vida" by Coldplay.

Who sang what:

Aiden Grimshaw – "Mad World" by Tears For Fears

Belle Amie – "Airplanes" by B.o.B

Cher Lloyd – "Just Be Good To Me" by Beats

International Diva Fever – "Sunny" by Bobby Hebb

FYD – "Billionaire" by Travie McCoy, featuring Bruno Mars

John Adeleye – "One Sweet Day" by Mariah Carey and Boyz II Men

Katie Waissel – "We Are The Champions" by Queen

Mary Byrne – "It's A Man's Man's Man's World" by James Brown

Matt Cardle – "When Love Takes Over" by David Guetta

Nicolo Festa – "Just Dance" by Lady Gaga

One Direction – "Viva La Vida" by Coldplay

Paije Richardson – "Killing Me Softly with His Song" by The Fugees

Rebecca Ferguson – "Teardrops" by Womack & Womack

Storm – "We Built This City" by Starship

Treyc Cohen – "One" by U2

Wagner – "She Bangs" and "Love Shack" medley by Ricky Martin and The B-52s

What the judges thought of One Direction's performance:

Louis: "Wow, guys, when I heard you were going to do Coldplay, I thought it was a big, big risk! I love what you did with the song—you totally made it your own. I love that the band is gelling. Even though Simon's going to claim he put this band together, it was my idea originally, Simon. It *was*! Boys, I think potentially you could be the next big boy band but you have a lot of work to do. But Simon, I'm not sure about the styling. Did you have a stylist?"

Dannii: "Guys, I don't know whose idea it was because I wasn't there, but you look like you fit together like you're the perfect band. That song was fantastic, and you did make it your own. I wasn't thinking of Coldplay then, it was the perfect pop band performance."

Cheryl: "I have to agree with Dannii, you look like you were meant to be together as a group. You look fantastic! You've got all the ingredients of the perfect pop band. I reckon the girls will be going crazy for you, but you need a little bit more time to develop as a group, that's all. Just a little bit more time."

Simon: "Regarding your role in putting the group together, Louis, we'll rewind the tapes on that one. You guys came together because your Bootcamp auditions weren't good enough but you were too good to throw away. We took a risk, and I've got to tell you, what was so impressive about that was when you started to screw up one of you at the end, Liam stepped in; you brought it back together. That's what bands do. Regarding the whole styling issue, Louis, I don't want to style this band because I don't know how to style a band like this. We asked the band to do whatever they wanted to do. I'm not going to interfere; they're going to do it their way. It was brilliant, guys!"

What the boys thought:

Liam and the boys were so happy that they weren't in the bottom two so they didn't need to worry about the sing-off. Now they could just look forward to the challenges of Week 2. Zayn told the backstage cameras: "We came off the stage after our performance, we were all buzzing. I don't know how to describe what it was like because you will never understand what it was like until you've actually performed on the stage. It was just amazing!"

The sing-off:

Nicolo Festa (from Dannii's Boys category) received the lowest vote so he automatically became the first act to leave the show. The sing-off was between Katie (from Cheryl's Girls category) and FYD (Simon's Groups category). Katie sang "Don't Let Me Down" by The Beatles and FYD sang Rihanna's "Please Don't Stop The Music." Simon voted to save his own act, FYD, but the other judges all voted for Katie to stay. FYD became the second act to leave the show.

Week 2 - Heroes

On October 16, the remaining fourteen acts had to sing songs from their musical heroes. One Direction chose to sing the Kelly Clarkson song, "My Life Would Suck Without You." It was an unusual choice for five teenage boys but considering Kelly won *American Idol*, it made perfect sense because they wanted to win *The X Factor*.

With just hours to go before the live show the boys had their soundcheck, but it didn't go well. When it was Harry's turn to sing, he found that he couldn't get the words out. He felt like he was going to be sick and the *X Factor* staff rushed him to see a doctor. It turned out that he wasn't suffering from an illness but it was a bad case of stage fright. Thankfully, by the time of the live show, he had managed to control his nerves and could sing again.

Who sang what:

Aiden Grimshaw – "Jealous Guy" by John Lennon

Belle Amie – "You Really Got Me" by The Kinks

Cher Lloyd – "Hard Knock Life" by Jay Z

Diva Fever – "Gotta Go Home/Barbra Streisand" by Boney M

John Adeleye – "A Song For You" by Donny Hathaway

Katie Waissel – "I'd Rather Go Blind" by Etta James

Mary Byrne – "You Don't Have To Say You Love Me" by Dusty Springfield

Matt Cardle – "Just The Way You Are" by Bruno Mars

One Direction – "My Life Would Suck Without You" by Kelly Clarkson

Paije Richardson – "If I Ain't Got You" by Alicia Keys

Rebecca Ferguson – "Feeling Good" by Nina Simone

Storm Lee – "Born To Run" by Bruce Springsteen

Treyc Cohen – "Purple Rain" by Prince

Wagner – "Help Yourself" by Tom Jones[

What the judges thought of One Direction's performance:

Louis: "Well, One Direction, you seem to be having fun on stage. I like the fact that you've gelled already. Every schoolgirl up and down the country is gonna love this. My only problem, boys, is with your mentor, Simon. Kelly Clarkson a hero? Simon, why? It was a strange song. Boys, you are really, really good, but I think Simon could've picked a better song."

Dannii: "Boys, maybe that's your musical hero. I have to say that you're five heartthrobs. You look great together, and Harry, whatever nerves you have, I'm sure that your friends and you stick together. The true measure of a boy band like you will be when you sing your big ballad, so I will be looking forward to hearing that."

Cheryl: "I can't even cope with how cute you are, seriously. I can't! I just want to go over and hug them, in a nice way. You're so sweet! I'm watching you the whole time, just thinking, *This is adorable.* But I want to be able to be saying, "Wow, this is the new big boy band!,' and I think that'll come in time."

Simon: "Okay, well, that time has just come. Let me tell you, you are the most exciting pop band in the country today. I'm being serious. There is something absolutely right."

What the boys thought:

Niall: "I think our performance went well last night. We had a good song, the crowd got behind us."

The boys were glad that Harry had managed to control his nerves but they weren't sure if they had done enough until host Dermot O'Leary announced that they had got through to Week 3.

The sing-off:

That week, two acts were eliminated. The first to go was the act with the lowest votes: Storm Lee. Following this, the acts with the second and third lowest votes had to face the sing-off. Simon's girl group, Belle Amie, sang "Big Girls Don't Cry" by Fergie and his wildcard group, Diva Fever, sang Gloria Gaynor's "I Will Survive." Louis, Dannii and Cheryl all voted to send home Diva Fever, meaning Simon didn't have to choose between his two groups.

Storm Lee became the third act and Diva Fever became the fourth act to leave the show.

Week 3 – Guilty Pleasures

For the third show on October 23, the remaining twelve acts had to sing songs that were described as their "guilty pleasures." The boys spent a week rehearsing one song, only to be told by Simon (with one day to go) that they needed to change to another one.

Who sang what:

Aiden Grimshaw – "Diamonds Are Forever" by Shirley Bassey

Belle Amie – "I'll Stand By You" by The Pretenders

Cher Lloyd – Mash up of "No Diggity" by Blackstreet and "Shout" by Tears for Fears

John Adeleye – "Zoom" by Fat Larry's Band

Katie Waissel – "I Wan'na Be Like You (The Monkey Song)" from *The Jungle Book*

Mary Byrne – "I Who Have Nothing" by Shirley Bassey

Matt Cardle – ". . . Baby One More Time" by Britney Spears

One Direction – "Nobody Knows" by Pink

Paije Richardson – "Ain't Nobody" by Chaka Khan

Rebecca Ferguson – "Why Don't You Do Right" by Nora Lee King

Treyc Cohen – "Whole Lotta Love" by Led Zeppelin

Wagner – Mash up of "Spice Up Your Life" by the Spice Girls and "Livin' La Vida Loca" by Ricky Martin

What the judges thought of One Direction's performance:

Louis: "You just have to walk out on the stage, everybody's screaming—it's like five Justin Biebers! And Liam, brilliant lead vocal from you! This band, you're really getting your act together. I think you are the next big pop band."

Dannii: "Being a band, everybody wants to live that dream with you. And it seems like you're living the dream, and loving the dream, and you're letting everyone in on that with you. Another great performance! I'm not sure why Pink is a guilty pleasure, though."

Cheryl: "You know what, guys? Let me just put this out there: you are my guilty pleasure. When you watch the TV and you see all the hysteria you caused when you went out there this week, that's what you should do. That's what boy bands should be about. Whenever The Beatles went anywhere, they caused that level of hysteria. You're finding your feet now, I'm looking forward to seeing you improve even more."

Simon: "With regards to the song, we chose a song, didn't work. But the good thing about you, guys, is that there's no bleating on about excuses—'I can't do this, I can't do that.' It's just a song. You grabbed hold of it within twenty-four hours, practiced. And I've got to tell you, apart from it being a great performance, I thought vocally, you've really, really made some really huge improvements. It's been an absolute pleasure working with you lot."

What the boys thought:

The boys found changing the song at the last minute quite stressful but they knew that Simon was right—the Pink song suited them better. Liam liked that it was a ballad because Dannii had wanted them to sing something slower and it showed the audience at home the wide variety of songs they could sing.

Harry told the backstage cameras: "The comments were absolutely brilliant! For us to keep proceeding in the competition we have to, we have to get better every week."

The boys also revealed that their top three guilty pleasure tracks are: John Travolta singing "Grease Lightning," "Tease Me" by Chaka Demus & Pliers and "I'm Too Sexy" by Right Said Fred.

The sing-off:

The two acts to receive the lowest votes were John Adeleye from Louis's Over-28s category and Treyc Cohen from Cheryl's Girls category. John chose to sing "Because Of You" by Kelly Clarkson and Treyc picked "One Night Only" from the musical, *Dream Girls*. Louis chose to save his act, John, but the other three judges picked Treyc.

John Adeleye became the fifth act to leave the show.

Week 4 – Halloween

On October 30, the final eleven acts had to sing a Halloween-themed song. All of them performed wearing scary costumes.

Who sang what:

Aiden Grimshaw – "Thriller" by Michael Jackson

Belle Amie – "Venus" by Bananarama

Cher Lloyd – "Stay" by Shakespears Sister

Katie Waissel – "Bewitched" by Steve Lawrence

Mary Byrne – "Could It Be Magic" by Barry Manilow

Matt Cardle – "Bleeding Love" by Leona Lewis

One Direction – "Total Eclipse Of The Heart" by Bonnie Tyler

Paije Richardson – "Back to Black" by Amy Winehouse

Rebecca Ferguson – "Wicked Game" by Chris Isaak

Treyc Cohen – "Relight My Fire" by Take That

Wagner – "O Fortuna/Bat Out of Hell" by Meat Loaf

What the judges thought of One Direction's performance:

Louis: "First, I was thinking, why were you picking this song? But it absolutely worked. I love the whole *Twilight*, vampire thing going in the background, and you definitely gel as a band. Everywhere I go, girls are saying, 'You know One Direction, tell One Direction I love them!' I think there's definitely something great about you; you definitely gel as friends. I love the way you all sing. Simon, it's definitely working. I'm not sure what the song's got to do with Halloween but guys, you're brilliant—keep doing it!"

Dannii: "Guys, like I've said before, you are a boy band doing exactly what a boy band should do. I'm looking at you and thinking the styling is even better than any other week. You make vampire hot—I want to come to your party!"

Cheryl: "It doesn't matter where I go, somebody, an older woman, young women, kids, everybody mentions One Direction. I think you have a really long way to go in this competition."

Simon: "Once again, a great performance. What I really admire about you guys is I know people are under pressure when you go into a competition like this—you've got to remember you're sixteen, seventeen years old, the way that you've conducted yourselves . . . Don't believe the hype, work hard, rehearse . . . Honestly, total pleasure working with you lot."

What the boys thought:

Harry told the backstage cameras on the Sunday: "Last night felt brilliant! We got a real chance to show off our vocals and hopefully the fans at home will vote and keep us in because we really don't want to go home now."

The boys were really grateful to have been given a classic song to sing because they felt it would appeal to a wide spectrum of people and some of the songs they had previously sung had been less well known.

The sing-off:

Cheryl's act, Katie Waissel, and Simon's girl group, Belle Amie, received the lowest number of votes so they had to take part in the sing-off. Katie chose to sing "Trust In Me" by Etta James and Belle Amie picked Kelly Clarkson's "Breakaway." Simon and Louis voted to send Katie home, with Dannii and Cheryl voting to send Belle Amie home. Because it was a draw the decision was left to the public vote and since Belle Amie received the fewest votes, they were sent home.

Belle Amie became the sixth act to leave the show.

Week 5 – American Anthems

The fifth week of *The X Factor* live shows saw the ten remaining acts sing American Anthems on November 6. By this point the boys were dreaming about possibly winning the show and Simon was doing his utmost to help them on their way. Simon thought that "Kids In America" was the perfect song for 1D and that their version could be a hit single, should it ever be released.

Who sang what:

Aiden Grimshaw – "Nothing Compares 2U" by Sinéad O'Connor

Cher Lloyd – "Empire State Of Mind" by Jay Z and Alicia Keys

Katie Waissel – "Don't Speak" by No Doubt

Mary Byrne – "There You'll Be" by Faith Hill

Matt Cardle – "The First Time Ever I Saw Your Face" by Roberta Flack

One Direction – "Kids In America" by Kim Wilde

Paije Richardson – Mash up of "I'm A Believer" by The Monkees and "Hey Ya!" by Outkast

Rebecca Ferguson – "Make You Feel My Love" by Bob Dylan

Treyc Cohen – "I Don't Want To Miss A Thing" by Aerosmith

Wagner – Mash up of "Viva Las Vegas" and "Wonder Of You" by Elvis Presley

What the judges thought of One Direction's performance:

Louis: "What a brilliant way to end the show! Listen, everywhere I go there's hysteria. It's building on this band. You remind me a bit of Westlife, Take That, Boyzone . . . You could be the next big band. I loved everything about the performance, but Simon, *Simon*, one point! I've had to get my rulebook out. The theme is "American Anthems"—this wasn't even a hit in America! It's by Kim Wilde . . . from London—it's not an American anthem, so you cheated. Your mentor has cheated."

Dannii: "It had the word 'America' in it, and it had American cheerleaders and it was a great performance, guys. I don't think vocally it was the best of the night, but a great performance."

Cheryl: "That absolutely cheered me up and brightened up my night! I thoroughly enjoyed that performance. You are great kids—I love chatting to you backstage, you are just good lads, nice lads. Great performance, good song choice . . . Cowell, I've got to give it to you, but it isn't American all the same."

Simon: "When you came out, it was like sunshine on a beautiful day, and I've said this before, and then 'Louis the Thundercloud' comes along and dribbles on everything that is happy. Taking all that rubbish to one side, because it was about the artist, it was about song title—that was without question your best performance by a mile."

What the boys thought:

The boys found performing "Kids In America" really fun. They liked having the cheerleaders with them and were very grateful to Brian Friedman, who had created the fantastic choreography. They loved having the opportunity to close the show, too.

The sing-off:

Katie Waissel and Treyc Cohen received the lowest number of votes and so they were in the sing-off (both acts were in Cheryl's category). Katie chose to sing "Please Don't Give Up On Me" by Solomon Burke and Treyc picked Toni Braxton's "Unbreak My Heart." Simon voted to send Treyc home, Cheryl controversially refused to vote, Dannii voted to send Katie home and Louis chose to send Treyc home. Cheryl had thought that *X Factor* host Dermot O'Leary would let the vote go to deadlock but this wasn't the case.

Because she had received two votes to go home, Treyc became the seventh act to leave *The X Factor*.

After the show, the boys were crushed to learn that some people thought they had been miming during their performance of "Kids In America." When the camera had focused in on Zayn it looked like he had missed his cue, even though you could still hear him sing. It wasn't actually Zayn's voice that you could hear, but Harry's, as he was singing at the time but because the camera was focused on Zayn, it made it look as though he was miming. That night poor Zayn was criticized a lot on Twitter and in the press.

RoseGardenAcs tweeted: "One Direction miming the chorus. I'd send them straight to the naughty step."

Alexander McNeil thought they were miming, too: "Zayn REALLY dropped the ball on The #xfactor tonight . . . so obviously One Direction were miming parts . . . ARGH!"

But the boys had given an amazing performance and should have been praised, not criticized. An *X Factor* spokesperson told the *Daily Mail*: "All Saturday night competitive performances are performed and sung live by the contestants.

"And we'd take it very seriously if there were any suggestion otherwise."

In fact the only time that the boys mimed was during the Sunday night show, when all the contestants performed one song together. The wannabe pop stars had to mime during that performance because they only had limited time to rehearse and all the songs were very high energy and involved a lot of movement. The general public couldn't vote after the group performances so these didn't impact on the final results.

Week 6 – Elton John

On November 13, the remaining nine acts had to sing Elton John songs. Liam, Zayn, Louis, Harry and Niall were a bit unsure at the beginning of the week when they were told the theme because they didn't know that many of Elton's numbers. In the end they decided to go for "Something About The Way You Look Tonight." Liam told the backstage cameras shortly before they went onstage: "This has easily been our best week yet and we'd like to end it with a great performance tonight."

Who sang what:

Aiden Grimshaw – "Rocket Man"

Cher Lloyd– Mash up of "Sorry Seems To Be The Hardest Word" and "Mockingbird" by Eminem

Katie Waissel – "Saturday Night's Alright For Fighting"

Mary Byrne – "Can You Feel The Love Tonight"

Matt Cardle – "Goodbye Yellow Brick Road"

One Direction – "Something About The Way You Look Tonight"

Paije Richardson – "Crocodile Rock"

Rebecca Ferguson – "Candle In The Wind"

Wagner – Mash up of "I'm Still Standing" and "Circle Of Life"

What the judges thought of One Direction's performance:

Louis: "Well, boys, after that performance I think you're only going in one direction . . . and that direction is the final! I talked to you guys a lot yesterday and I really got to know you. I know that you're taking the whole thing really, really seriously and, you know, going to be the next big boy band and you've gelled as friends, and I've nothing but good to say about One Direction!"

Dannii: "Guys, you are so consistent, it's scary! That song could have been really boring but it was great. That's what I would love to hear you sing at your concerts, which I'm sure you will be doing one day."

[Crowd cheers]

Cheryl: "Listen to that! That's what it's about . . . to hear that is the measure of what you've become so you definitely are heading in one direction."

Simon: "Guys, I want to say something, okay? This is the first time in all the years of *X Factor* where I genuinely believe a group are going to win this competition. And you know what, I want to say this: what was so impressive, you've seen the girls and anything else, you've remained focused, you've been really nice to the crew, you're nice to the fans and most importantly, everything that happened tonight, from the choice of song to what they wore, it was all down to you. Guys, congratulations!"

What the boys thought:

Liam and the boys were blown away by the judges' comments. Having to sing out of their comfort zone had been a positive thing rather than a negative.

Louis told the official *X Factor* website: "Last night was absolutely incredible, the crowd were amazing!" Zayn added: "The competition's really, really heating up."

The sing-off:

Cheryl's act, Katie Waissel, and Dannii's act, Aiden Grimshaw, received the lowest number of votes so they had to sing for survival. Aiden had been the favorite to win the whole show so the audience watching at home and in the studio were shocked. Katie chose to sing "Save Me From Myself" by Christina Aguilera and Aiden picked Crowded

House's "Don't Dream It's Over." Simon and Cheryl both voted to send Aiden home, with Dannii and Louis voting to send Katie home. It all came down to the public vote and because Aiden received the least number of votes he became the eighth act to leave the show.

Eighteen-year-old Aiden Grimshaw from Blackpool was one of the boys' closest friends on *The X Factor* and they were devastated when he was told he was going home. While Aiden and Katie prepared to sing for survival in the advertising break, One Direction's Louis tweeted: "What a joke Wagner through and not Aiden!!! Aiden has to get through!!!!"

After the result he angrily tweeted: "Not only was he one of my best friends, he was one of the best singers in the competition, yet people who can't sing a note in tune are still here. Wow."

And the boys weren't the only ones to be upset and angered after Aiden's *X Factor* dream was over. His mentor Dannii Minogue tweeted: "My utmost respect to Aiden. I have loved working with him on *X Factor*. TeamMinogue will miss him and I wish him the VERY BEST! Dx"

Week 7 – The Beatles

The seventh week of *The X Factor* live shows took place on November 20 and saw the eight remaining acts singing songs by The Beatles. Liam told the show's official website shortly before their performance: "I'm a massive fan of The Beatles and I'm really looking forward to tonight. Although it's an oldie, we're going to make the song we sing tonight feel current. It's a complicated performance for us, full of harmonies and adlibs, but it's the sort of performance that I think you'd expect from a top boy band. We're feeling the pressure a bit, but if it all goes to plan, it'll be awesome!"

Who sang what:

Cher Lloyd – "Imagine" by John Lennon

Katie Waissel – "Help!"

Mary Byrne – "Something"

Matt Cardle – "Come Together"

One Direction – "All You Need Is Love"

Paije Richardson – "Let It Be"

Rebecca Ferguson – "Yesterday"

Wagner – Mash up of "Get Back," "Hippy Hippy Shake" and "Hey Jude"

What the judges thought of One Direction's performance:

Louis: "Hey, One Direction, thank God for you guys! You lifted the whole energy in the studio. Good to see the Fab Five singing the Fab Four. The hysteria here has lifted your game—you are in it for the long haul, yes!"

Dannii: "Guys, another fantastic performance! I've always given you good comments—I just have to say tonight you guys (Niall and Zayn) were struggling. I don't know if it was caught on camera, but you were struggling with the backing vocals. You didn't know if you were coming in or out. Don't let the other guys down—you have to work as a group."

Cheryl: "I could get into the whole, 'I don't know why your mentor put you on a plain platform like that' but I won't because above everything else, that was another great performance from you guys."

Simon: "Who cares about the platform? Can I just say, guys, as always, you worked hard, delivered a fantastic, unique version of the song and please, for anyone at home who saw what happened last week, please don't think these guys are safe. This lot [Louis, Dannii and Cheryl] do not want you to do well in the competition. I do . . . please vote."

Cheryl had criticized the boys standing on a platform because earlier in the show Simon had criticized her decision to place Cher Lloyd on a staircase for her performance of "Imagine." It was all very petty.

What the boys thought:

Niall believed it was their best performance to date, while Liam told the backstage cameras: "Dannii gave us a bad comment but we're going to get bad comments so we've just got to take it on board and improve it next week."

The sing-off:

Cheryl's act, Katie Waissel, and Dannii's act, Paije Richardson, received the lowest number of votes so they had to sing for survival. Katie chose to sing "Stay" by Shakespears

Sister and Paije picked Sam Brown's "Stop." Dannii voted to send Katie home, with the other three judges all voting to send Paije home.

Paije became the ninth act to leave the show.

Week 8 – Rock Week

On November 27, the theme was Rock and the remaining seven acts had to sing two rock-themed songs each. Having to sing two songs rather than one put all the acts under extra pressure, but especially 1D because they had to sort out harmonies. At the last minute everyone learned that two acts would be leaving the show instead of just one. The act that received the fewest votes would automatically go and then the second and third from the bottom would have to sing again.

Who sang what:

Cher Lloyd – "Girlfriend" by Avril Lavigne, "Walk This Way" by Run DMC/Aerosmith

Katie Waissel – "Sex On Fire" by Kings Of Leon, "Everybody Hurts" by R.E.M.

Mary Byrne – "All I Want Is You" by U2, "Brass In Pocket" by The Pretenders

Matt Cardle – "I Love Rock'n'Roll" by Joan Jett and the Blackhearts, "Nights In White Satin" by The Moody Blues

One Direction – "Summer Of 69" by Bryan Adams, "You Are So Beautiful" by Joe Cocker

Rebecca Ferguson - "I Still Haven't Found What I'm Looking For" by U2, "I Can't Get No Satisfaction" by Aretha Franklin

Wagner - "Creep" by Radiohead, "Addicted To Love" by Robert Palmer

What the judges thought of One Direction's performances:

Performance 1 – "Summer of 69"

Louis: "Hey, boys, that absolutely worked! I love the choice of song, I love the vibe, the vitality you bring to the competition . . . The competition would not be the same without One Direction. I love the way that you've gelled as friends. I think you're the next big boy band."

Dannii: "You've clearly done lots of work and really stepped it up - I like that."

Cheryl: "We've got feet stamps going on, there's electricity in the room—it's fantastic! You just keep growing and growing, and getting better and better. I think there's a big future for you, congratulations."

Simon: "I had nothing to do with this song choice— Harry chose the song, great choice of song. Just remember next week is the semifinal. You've worked your butts off to get where you've got to—you've got to be there next week. Please pick up the phone."

Performance 2 – "You Are So Beautiful"

Louis: "Wow, boys! You've proven tonight you're not just another boy band–you're a brilliant, brilliant vocal group and you've proved that everybody in this group can sing. Which is incredible. I love the song; I love everything about it. I don't think it's a rock song, Simon, it's in the rules, but it is a brilliant song. It's not really a rock song, is it?"

Dannii: "Guys, there's one word for that and that's stunning. Absolutely wonderful!"

Cheryl: "It's great to see you having fun, and having all the dancers and all of that. I love that side of you, but I absolutely loved you standing and hearing you sing. It's what it's all about. You should be able to do everything and I think you've got a really bright future as a boy band, I really do."

Simon: "This was in some ways my favorite performance by you because it was beautifully sung and Zayn in particular, I can remember back at Bootcamp and I had to get you from the back because you were too embarrassed to dance, and I've seen how you've transformed, found your confidence and how the boys have looked after you. Genuinely, I am so proud of you tonight, congratulations."

What the boys thought:

While the boys hoped they had done enough, they couldn't be sure. They ended up being the last act to be named by host Dermot O'Leary as having a guaranteed place in the semifinal. Louis confided in the *Doncaster Today* that before their name was called, he thought they wouldn't be safe. He said: "All I remember thinking was that we needed to smash our "save me" song so that we could stay in the competition. We don't know from week to week if we are going to get through because there's been a lot of surprises."

After the boys had left the stage Niall jumped high in the air "like a kangaroo" according to Louis, and the boys all celebrated with their families.

Louis added: "The pressure is really on, we've not had a minute. We're constantly working and improving our vocals. We've been doing eighteen-hour days and have been in the studio until two am, so it's really tough."

The sing-off:

Katie Waissel received the fewest votes so she was automatically sent home. Louis's two acts, Wagner and Mary Byrne, were in the sing-off. Wagner chose to sing "Unforgettable" by Nat King Cole, while Mary picked Shirley Bassey's "This Is My Life." Wagner had had a great run, but his time had come to a close. Louis, Dannii and Cheryl chose to send him home so Simon didn't have to vote, but if he had then he, too, would have sent Wagner home.

Wagner became the eleventh act to leave the show.

Week 9 – Semi-final

For the semi-final on December 4 the final five acts had

to perform two songs. The first had to be a Club Classic and the second could be any song at all so long as it would cause people at home to pick up their phones and vote for them.

Who sang what:

Cher Lloyd – "Nothin' On You" by B.O.B, "Love The Way You Lie" by Eminem

Mary Byrne – "Never Can Say Goodbye" by Gloria Gaynor, "The Way We Were" by Barbra Streisand

Matt Cardle – "You've Got The Love" by Florence + The Machine, "She's Always A Woman" by Fyfe Dangerfield

One Direction – "Only Girl In The World" by Rihanna, "Chasing Cars" by Snow Patrol

Rebecca Ferguson – "Show Me Love" by Steve Angelo, "Amazing Grace" (Susan Boyle version)

What the judges thought of One Direction's performances:

Performance 1 – "Only Girl In The World"

Louis: "Week after week, you're getting better and better and you bring hysteria to the show. If there is any justice you will absolutely be in the final—you deserve to be in the final! I think you're the next big boy band and you know, guys, I love the way you've gelled. I know you're best friends and you've got something special."

Dannii: "Guys, I hope you never let us down because I really wanna see you guys as the next big boy band. I have to say, some weeks you come out and I think it's very samey.

That one was brilliant, you really stepped it up for the semi-finals. Brilliant!"

Cheryl: "Okay, first of all I'm gonna say I love you guys. This week, for me, I got to know you all a little bit better because your mentor wasn't here. I thoroughly enjoyed mentoring you, thank you for that opportunity, but that song for me was a little bit dangerous because it's so current right now as Rihanna's record that you have to completely make it like it was never, ever written for her and I don't know if it quite worked for me but I don't think it makes a difference. I hope to see you in the final."

Simon: "Someone's being tactical [referring to Cheryl's comments]. I've got to tell you, guys, I know this is going to sound a little bit biased but I thought the song was absolutely perfect for you because it is exactly what I liked about them: they didn't take the safe option. They chose something completely different; they had the guts to do it. I thought you looked current, sounded current and standing by what Cheryl said, you guys are just fantastic to work with. Can I just say, you hear all the applause and people at home might think you're safe, but nobody is safe in this competition and I would urge anyone, please, if they want to see these boys in the final, please pick up the phone and vote for them because they deserve it."

Performance 2 – "Chasing Cars"

Louis: "Liam, Zayn, Niall, Harry and Louis, I know your names! Guys, there's something about this band—you've definitely got something special. I think you're the next big boy band, but I said that last week. I loved the song choice, I loved the whole styling, I love the fact that you're really good friends. There's a great vibe about you. If there's any justice all the young kids will pick up their phones and they're going to vote One Direction—you deserve it!"

Dannii: "Guys, you've got through a really tough week and that was such a classy, classy performance! You've just grown up in front of our eyes and we've never, ever had such a good band on *The X Factor*—so proud to see you perform on this show."

Cheryl: "I know me, personally, all the crew, all the staff . . . everybody has grown so fond of you guys over the last few weeks. This week I was so impressed. You didn't have Zayn, Simon wasn't around, you showed a real level of maturity and you really deserve a place in the final."

Simon: "Guys, Tim who's been working with you all week told me that you made a decision this morning to get in at eight in the morning so you could give yourselves more rehearsal time and that's what it's all about. It's not about excuses, it's about having that great work ethic, picking yourselves up after what was a very tough week, and I said this before, I genuinely mean this: I am proud of you as people as much as I am artists. That was a great performance, good for you!"

The sing-off:

Cheryl's act, Cher Lloyd, and Louis's act, Mary Byrne, were in the bottom two and had to sing for a place in the final. Cher chose to sing Britney Spears's "Everytime" and Mary picked the song she had sung in Week 1, "It's A Man's Man's Man's World" by James Brown. Louis voted to save Mary, but the other three judges voted for Cher to stay.

Mary became the thirteenth person to leave the show.

Zayn loved performing on stage every weekend, singing with his new friends. Every Sunday when host Dermot O'Leary announced who was safe and who was in the bottom two he felt a mixture of emotions—waiting for him to say that One Direction were through was torture. Every time he did, Zayn would hug the others and Simon—the boys couldn't help but jump up and down with relief and happiness.

Not everything about Zayn's *X Factor* journey was good, though. His grandad died a few days before the semifinal and Zayn was left heartbroken. He had been ill for a while but Zayn was still shocked when he heard the news. He rushed home to Bradford to be with his family but made it back for the live show on the Saturday night. Zayn's grandad had been so proud of how well his grandson and the other boys had been doing on the show. At the funeral the boys' version of "You Are So Beautiful" was played—it was Zayn's grandad's favorite song. Because Zayn was so busy with *The X Factor* and being in 1D he didn't have time to grieve properly, but eventually, months down the line, he did.

All the *X Factor* judges were supportive of the boys, even though, for some, they were competing against their own acts.

During an interview the boys did for the *X Factor* website Liam said: "Being on stage is absolutely amazing! I mean, we only spend such a short time on it but we love absolutely every second of it. We wouldn't change any of it, it's great!"

Zayn added: "This for us is just unbelievable! We were all sat in the car today and I think it was Liam that said, 'It feels like a dream and that we're all going to wake up, and our mums are gonna be like, *Wake up, get ready for school!* kind of thing.' "

Along with the other acts, the boys released a charity single during their time on *The X Factor* which was released at the end of October 2010. It was a cover of David Bowie's "Heroes" and the money raised went to the Help for Heroes charity. The boys visited Headley Court Military Rehabilitation Center to meet some recovering soldiers and understand a bit more about what they go through once they return to the UK. The single was a big hit and was Number 1 in the UK charts.

When they filmed the video the boys were joined in the studio by some of the people Help for Heroes have assisted. Liam told a reporter from *The Sun*: "I can't believe some of the people who fight out there are younger than me. It's so shocking that people our age can come back from places like Afghanistan disabled forever. We're all really active in the band—we play football and work out all the time. The thought of not being able to do that is horrible."

Niall added: "It really puts things into perspective. We all complained about having to get up early and do this video shoot this morning—I feel so bad about that now. You don't realize how lucky you are. We're doing a huge TV show and other people have really, really tough jobs."

The boys loved filming the video and performing the track on *The X Factor* live show a few days later. When it went to Number 1 Zayn told Radio 1 host Reggie Yates: "It was pretty crazy when we were told we got to Number 1. Because it's for such a good cause and something we're all really proud about, that makes it so much better."

It took nine weeks (and eleven amazing performances) for Zayn, Niall, Liam, Louis and Harry to make *The X Factor* final and compete for the recording deal on offer. Their rivals for the title of *X Factor* winners 2010 were Rebecca Ferguson, Cher Lloyd and Matt Cardle. In the days leading up to the final the remaining contestants got to enjoy a day in their respective hometowns, or in One Direction's case, a few hours in the home towns of Harry, Louis, Zayn and Liam. Sadly for Niall they were unable to make the trip over to Ireland in case they got snowed in and couldn't fly back for the final.

The first thing they did was head out to a TV studio to do a live link with Ireland AM so that One Direction's Irish fans wouldn't miss out, and then they traveled to Doncaster to visit Louis's old school. After a brief visit the boys jumped in their car and traveled to Holmes Chapel, Cheshire, where Harry is from (it was also where they got to know each other in the weeks before the Judges' Houses round). Zayn and the boys enjoyed a small party at Harry's family home before traveling to Zayn's home town of Bradford. Rather than visit his school or the family home, they headed for the city center and the HMV music store. Hundreds of people lined the street, all desperate to see Zayn. He couldn't get over the reception—only a few months earlier he'd been able to walk down the street, unrecognized. Zayn admitted to the others that he would love to do an album signing in the store one day. Before long, the boys needed to be on the move again as they had a show to put on in Liam's home town of Wolverhampton. They met Simon there and performed three songs for the waiting fans who had come out to show their support.

The boys were so tired that night once they got back to the *X Factor* house and crawled into their beds. They had clocked up many miles but Zayn and the others thought it had been completely worth it just to see the smiles on the faces of the fans in Bradford, Doncaster, Holmes Chapel and Wolverhampton. Now they needed to rest as much as they could until the Saturday night and then if they got through, think about the Sunday night. They were about to have the busiest weekend of their lives so far.

Saturday – Who sang what – Song 1:

One Direction – "Your Song" by Elton John

Cher Lloyd – Mash up of "369" by Cupid Ft B.o.B and "Get Your Freak On" by Missy Elliott

Matt Cardle – "Here With Me" by Dido

Rebecca Ferguson – "Like A Star" by Corinne Bailey Rae

What the judges thought of One Direction's performance:

Louis Walsh: "Hey, One Direction, you're in the final! I hope you're here tomorrow night. It's amazing how five guys have gelled so well. I know you're all best friends. I've never seen a band cause so much hysteria so early in their caree—I definitely think that you've got an amazing future. Niall, everybody in Ireland must vote for Niall, yes!"

Dannii Minogue: "Guys, you have worked so hard in this competition. You were thrown together, you deserve to be here and I'd love to see you in the final tomorrow."

Cheryl Cole: "You know what? I have thoroughly enjoyed watching you guys growing every week, having the most amount of fun possible, and I think that you deserve to be standing on that stage tomorrow night."

Simon Cowell: "I just would like to say after hearing the first two performances tonight—Matt and Rebecca—they were so good, my heart was sinking. And then you came up on stage . . . You've got to remember that you're sixteen, seventeen years old, and each of you proved that you should be there as individual singers—you gave it 1,000 percent. It's been an absolute pleasure working with you. I really hope people bother to pick up the phone, put you through to tomorrow, because you deserve to be there."

Saturday – Who sang what
Song 2 – The Duets:

One Direction – "She's The One" with Robbie Williams

Cher Lloyd – Mash up of "Where Is The Love" and "I Gotta Feeling" with Will.i.am

Matt Cardle – "Unfaithful" with Rihanna

Rebecca Ferguson – "Beautiful" with Christina Aguilera

What the Boys Thought:

Zayn loved singing with Robbie Williams in the final because he'd spent time getting to know the boys during the day—he didn't just show up at the last minute to sing. For Louis and Niall it was a dream come true because they are huge fans.

For the duet the boys wore brightly colored suits and stood with Liam on the left, then Niall, Harry in the middle, then Louis, with Zayn on the right-hand side. Zayn's suit was green and he wore a black shirt—he looked absolutely gorgeous. Liam started the singing and then Harry took over before Zayn, Niall and Louis joined in with "She's the One." Their harmonies were perfect. The audience must have been wondering where Robbie was, but he appeared as soon as Louis said: "Right, there's a man who is a hero to all of us. Here he is, the incredible Robbie Williams!"

So, Robbie joined the lineup, standing between Harry and Louis. Zayn might not have been into Robbie's music all that much before but he was happy as they sang together—he was bopping along in between his singing parts. Robbie high-fived them all and at the end of their performance they had a group hug.

The boys were so grateful that Robbie had been willing to sing with them and Simon thanked him personally, saying: "Robbie is a great friend to the show—very, very generous with his time and he's made these boys' night of their lives! Thank you, Robbie."

The Result:

Every result show had been extremely tense but it was even more nerve-wracking for Zayn as he waited with the boys and Simon to find out if they had done enough to make Sunday's final show or whether they would be going home in fourth place. The first name that host Dermot O'Leary called out was Rebecca Ferguson—she was the first act safe. Next, he called One Direction and Zayn couldn't believe it. After jumping up and down, the boys hugged Simon—they were so excited! The final act to be joining them was Matt Cardle, which meant that Cher Lloyd had reached the end of the road and would be leaving that night.

Sunday – Who sang what:

One Direction sang "Torn" by Natalie Imbruglia

Matt Cardle sang "Firework" by Katy Perry

Rebecca Ferguson sang "Sweet Dreams" by Eurythmics

What the judges thought of One Direction's performance:

Louis Walsh: "One Direction, you're in the final! You could be the first band to win *The X Factor*—it's up to the public at home but you've got brilliant chemistry. I love the harmonies, I love the song choice and we've got five new pop stars!"

Dannii Minogue: "Guys, you've done all the right things to make your place here in the final. That was a fantastic performance! Whatever happens tonight, I'm sure you guys are going to go on and release records and be the next big band."

Cheryl Cole: "It's been so lovely to watch you guys from your first audition—to think that was only a few months ago. I really believe that you've got a massive future ahead of you and I wanna say thank you for being such lovely guys to be around. It's been great getting to know you and good luck with the show tonight."

Simon Cowell: "Let's be clear, anyone who comes into this final has got a great chance of bettering their future. But this is a competition and in terms of the competition, in terms of who's worked the hardest, who I think deserves to win based on the future of something we haven't seen before, I would love to hear your names read out at the end of the competition because I think you deserve it."

The Result:

There were two results on the Sunday night: the first to find out who had come third and the second to announce who had won *The X Factor 2010*. Waiting for the results on the Saturday night had been intense but time seemed to stand still for the first results of the Sunday show. The first name *X Factor* host Dermot O'Leary called was Matt Cardle so it was either One Direction or Rebecca Ferguson who had finished in third place. Sadly for Zayn, Harry, Niall, Liam and Louis, it was Rebecca who was named as the second act to go through to the last part of the show: they had finished in third place.

The boys' mentor, Simon Cowell, appeared to be utterly disappointed and immediately turned his back, hiding his face from the cameras. Devastated, Zayn and the other boys were trying their hardest not to cry; they had come so close. As they went over to congratulate Rebecca, Zayn was slightly behind the others—he was so upset. They watched the video montage of their *X Factor* journey before host Dermot asked what for them had been the highlight. Louis said: "It's been absolutely incredible. For me, the highlight was when we first sang together at Judges' Houses, that was unbelievable and you know what? We've done our absolute best, we've worked hard."

Zayn added: "We're definitely going to stay together, this isn't the last of One Direction!"

Simon agreed with Zayn, saying: "I'm absolutely gutted for them, but look, for everyone who has bothered to pick up the phone over the past few weeks, I really appreciate it and all I can say is this is just the beginning!"

Following this, the boys had to leave the stage with Simon as the two remaining contestants, Matt Cardle and Rebecca Ferguson, had one more song each to sing. They had to sing the song they would release, should they win. It must have been so hard on the boys because they had prepared a song, too, but they didn't get the opportunity to perform it.

Later on in the show Dermot O'Leary announced that Matt was the winner and Rebecca was runner-up. The boys were happy for Matt because they had become close to him during their *X Factor* journey. All along they had insisted that if they didn't win, they wanted him to do so.

After the show, Zayn, Harry, Niall, Liam and Louis tweeted from their official Twitter account: "Congratulations Matt! Please support Matt by buying When We Collide . . . iTunes."

Through taking part in *The X Factor* the boys had had the opportunity to meet lots of singers and bands, including JLS, The Wanted, Westlife and Take That. Zayn and his bandmates were able to see how other boy bands work and play together. The different bands all offered the boys advice about how the music industry works and spelled out how important it is be friends as well as bandmates.

Even though Zayn and the boys didn't win, they soon had something to smile about when Simon offered them a record deal. He told them to meet him in his office and the next day offered them a £2 million ($2.9 million) recording contract with his company, Syco. *X Factor* winner Matt

Cardle had secured a £1 million ($1.4 million) recording contract so the boys actually did better by not winning! They were sworn to secrecy because Simon didn't want the news getting out straightaway—it wouldn't have been fair on Matt or the other *X Factor* acts who hadn't yet secured deals.

Zayn told *The X Factor Australia*: "When we got to the final, we were like, we want to win this . . . we got kicked out, we came third. At the time we were massively disappointed.

"The next day, Simon called us into the Sony offices and we signed a contract so that was crazy!"

In fact, Simon Cowell isn't so scary as he is often portrayed. Zayn described what he was like as a mentor to New Zealand radio hosts Jay-Jay, Mike and Dom. He said: "He was very different to what we thought he was going to be like because obviously he gets portrayed as this massively scary figure who's like, the head of the music industry, and we met him and he's such a cool, down-to-earth guy . . . You can talk to him about football, girls and he's really cool, and he's stayed completely faithful to us. He took full control of the One Direction campaign and everything."

Here is a list of the acts that performed as part of the results shows:

Week 1 – Joe McElderry and Usher

Week 2 – Diana Vickers and Katy Perry

Week 3 – Cheryl Cole and Michael Bublé

Week 4 – Jamiroquai and Rihanna

Week 5 – Shayne Ward and Kylie Minogue

Week 6 – JLS, Westlife and Take That

Week 7 – Olly Murs

Week 8 – The Wanted, Justin Bieber and Nicole Scherzinger

Week 9 – Alexandra Burke, the cast of *Glee* and The Black Eyed Peas

Week 10 – Rihanna and Christina Aguilera

Once the final was over, Zayn, Harry, Liam, Louis and Niall had some promo gigs to do around the UK. Their first shows were in Scotland, and the boys had to quickly adapt to performing on a small stage in front of a few hundred people. Performing in clubs was a strange experience as only Louis was really old enough to be there as he was the only one who was eighteen (Zayn and Liam were seventeen and Harry and Niall were sixteen). Most of the time the audiences were made up of girls who had supported Zayn and the boys throughout their *X Factor* journey, but they did occasionally receive boos from lads in the audience who were jealous of their success.

Once they had finished the gigs in various parts of the UK, Zayn was finally able to go home for Christmas and enjoy spending time with his family. He bought his sister Doniya a pair of Ugg boots—she had wanted them for ages but they had been out of her price range. For New Year's Eve he partied with friends. It was nice to be plain old Zayn again and not Zayn from The X Factor. But he could only stay in Bradford for a short time –he now had to move permanently to London, something that was hard on both Zayn and his family. Mum Trisha would have liked nothing more than for her son to move back home into his old bedroom but at the same time she was delighted that he was living his dream

CHAPTER FIVE

UP ALL NIGHT

2011 was a huge year for Zayn, Harry, Niall, Liam and Louis, and they were really busy from the very start. First, they had The X Factor Live Tour to look forward to, which went to the major arenas around the UK and Ireland, and then they had to work on their debut album, *Up All Night*.

Before tour rehearsals began, the boys had to get their passports out again and fly to Los Angeles to start choosing songs and recording with legendary record producer RedOne. Zayn was really nervous about flying and the other boys teased him ruthlessly.

He was also overwhelmed that they had been given the opportunity to work with RedOne (real name Nadir Khayat) because he had worked with Michael Jackson on his final album, *Invincible*, and had also collaborated with big stars like Lady Gaga, Nicole Scherzinger, Backstreet Boys and Cher. Zayn believes RedOne helped give an anthemic vibe to *Up All Night*. He told the *Daily Star*: "To work with RedOne was such a big deal. It's more like the sound he created with Nicole Scherzinger. Powerful."

While in LA, Zayn actually saw his first concert with his fellow bandmates, as they all went together to see Britney Spears. The other boys had been attending concerts for many years: for Niall and Louis, their first was Busted, for Liam, it was seeing the *Pop Idol* finalists and for Harry, it was Nickelback.

Simon Cowell didn't want to keep the fans waiting too long for the first One Direction album and the boys were eager to start recording tracks, too. Sonny Takhar, the chief executive officer of Syco Records, explained to *Music Week*: "We started working with the band immediately after the show had finished—they went to LA and recorded with RedOne. Then, while the boys were out on The X Factor Tour between February and April, we started finding and sourcing songs and creating situations where songs were written for the boys in preparation for them to record once they had finished."

Zayn loved how warm it was in America—it had been really cold in the run-up to Christmas in the UK so it was nice to be back wearing T-shirts and shorts again. The boys didn't have that much time to sunbathe and enjoy the sights because their schedules were pretty tightly packed but Zayn still managed to fit in a few shopping trips. He loves high-top sneakers so picked up a nice pair of black Nike ones as a treat. Back then, he could stroll around Los Angeles without being recognized, but of course there is no way he could do that today—he'd get mobbed!

Looking good matters to Zayn and he loves being fashionable. He was the *X Factor* contestant who spent the longest time in front of the mirror and later topped *MyCelebrityFashion.co.uk*'s list of the Best Dressed Celebrity Males of 2013. Previously, the title had been held by Harry Styles in 2012 but this time he dropped to fourth in the 2013 list. In second place was radio DJ Nick Grimshaw, David Beckham was third and in fifth place came Chris Brown.

The boys were only in Los Angeles for a few days before they had to fly back to the UK to attend rehearsals for the tour. Singing to up to 20,000 people each night was to be a new experience for them. Zayn's family couldn't wait to go and see the guys perform. Meanwhile, the bandmates had to learn how to fill the stage and perform some dance moves during their songs, so there was a lot to take in. They weren't too apprehensive, though, because the other *X Factor* acts also had to learn everything from scratch and it would be nicely relaxing to hang out with them, especially since they hadn't seen many of them since the *X Factor* wrap party.

Zayn, Niall, Liam, Louis and Harry performed five songs during each concert: "Only Girl," "Chasing Cars," "Kids In America," "My Life Would Suck Without You" and a song called "Forever Young" by 80s synth-pop group Alphaville, which would have been their first single, had they won *The X Factor*. The first show was at Birmingham's LG Arena on February 19 and the finale would take place at Motorpoint Arena Cardiff (formerly known as Cardiff International Arena) on April 9, 2011.

Once the tour was over, Zayn and the boys had to say goodbye to many of the acts, for those who hadn't managed to secure a recording deal would go back to their normal lives. But the bandmates wouldn't have many opportunities to socialize with the people who were staying on in London because they were going to be very busy.

Zayn had loved being on the tour but getting back in the recording studio was even better. He learned so much from the amazing songwriters and record producers they were working with and the boys had a blast, eating takeout and messing around when they could. They had to work hard, but they were allowed to enjoy themselves, too. Of course spending so much time together led to the occasional rift but if Zayn ever had an argument with any of the boys, he'd buy them all takeout to make up for it!

Looking back, they freely admit that with *Up All Night* they didn't have much say in which songs made up the album. They also had to work on their pronunciation, as the producers wanted everything to be perfect. They couldn't just go into a studio and record a song in an hour—it took a long time to get everything right.

A love of English from a young age meant that Zayn was also interested in poetry and he felt that the songs they were writing were like poetry set to music. He loved having the opportunity to cowrite songs and put his own stamp on them. The boys flew out to Los Angeles again and they also spent some time recording in Sweden.

During their stint on *The X Factor* the boys had received vocal training from Savan Kotecha, one of the world's best vocal coaches. Also a talented songwriter, Kotecha has written songs for Britney Spears, Leona Lewis, Westlife, Usher and many more international stars. After *The X Factor* wrapped, he was asked whether he would be interested in writing songs for One Direction and he jumped at the chance. He enjoyed working with Zayn, Harry, Niall, Liam and Louis—he found them full of energy and eager to learn. During *The X Factor*, he had written a funny song for them called "Vas Happenin' Boys." In it, he sings about Harry being a slob and needing to win *The X Factor* because he can't get a job and says that Harry's dad could be Mick Jagger. He also sings that Zayn is the master of echoes, Louis needs a boat, Niall was raised by leprechauns and Liam looks sad when he sings. To hear the song for yourself, check it out on YouTube—Savan and the boys had lots of fun filming it.

On the boys' first album, *Up All Night*, Savan cowrote "What Makes You Beautiful," "I Wish," "One Thing," "Na Na Na," "Up All Night" and "Save You Tonight." Other songwriters and producers who worked on the album included the award-winning producer and songwriter Steve Robson, who has worked with Take That, Faith Hill, James Martin, Olly Murs, Leona Lewis and many more world-class performers. Robson cowrote "Everything About You" and "Same Mistakes" with songwriter Wayne Hector, who has written songs for Nicki Minaj, The Wanted and Westlife and has had over thirty Number 1 hits—quite an achievement. The producer of Britney Spears's ". . . Baby One More Time," Rami Yacoub, also worked on the boys' first album, cowriting "What Makes You Beautiful," "I Wish" and "One Thing" with Savan Kotecha and Carl Falk (Falk cowrote the record-breaking "Starships" for Nicki Minaj).

Originally two songs, the songwriters decided to take the chorus from one song and the verses from the other to create "One Thing." It is Carl Falk's favorite track on the album—he likes it even more than the boys' first single, "What Makes You Beautiful."

Out of the fifteen tracks on *Up All Night* (thirteen on the standard version, plus the two tracks on the *Limited Yearbook* edition of the album), Zayn's favorite has to be "Tell Me A Lie," which was written by Kelly Clarkson. Altogether, he has approximately five-and-a-half minutes of solos and if he had to sum up the album in one word, he would pick "anthemic."

Zayn was so excited when he could walk into any record store in the UK and buy *Up All Night*! The album was released in Ireland on November 18, 2011 and three days later in the UK. His family and friends were all so proud of him and rushed out to buy multiple copies. To have charted at Number 1 in Ireland was a dream come true for the boys, especially Niall. The album peaked at Number 2 in the

UK after selling 138,163 copies in the first week of release and it did even better worldwide when released in 2012. It was released in America on March 13, 2013 and debuted at Number 1 on the *Billboard* 200 album chart, selling 176,000 copies in the first week.

One Direction were the first UK/Ireland group to get to Number 1 in America with their debut album, an amazing achievement. What was really positive was that the boys were in New York when they released the album and so they could celebrate with fans at album signings in the city. They had actually decided to bring the album out a week earlier than planned because their fans were desperate to listen to it. Zayn was actually in bed when he got the phone call to say they were Number 1, desperately trying to catch up on some sleep after all the nonstop promotion.

As well as being a huge hit in the States, the album was Number 1 in Australia, Canada, Croatia, Italy, Mexico, New Zealand and Sweden.

To Zayn and the other boys being Number 1 in so many countries just didn't feel real, it felt like they were dreaming, but they didn't have much time to celebrate because their schedules were so packed.

Zayn's former teachers were so proud of him when they heard that *Up All Night* had reached Number 1 in the US. John Edwards, head teacher of Lower Fields Primary, told the *Telegraph & Angus*: "It's brilliant. The thing that impresses me about Zayn is that fame hasn't changed him one bit. He pops into school every so often. He is totally unaffected, respectful, a delightful young man. It couldn't have happened to a nicer person.

"We followed him closely through the competition [*The X Factor*] and we were delighted when they were so successful, but never envisaged it would become a worldwide phenomenon."

The head teacher of Zayn's high school, Steve Curran, also told the newspaper: "We are delighted and proud of Zayn's success and would like to congratulate One Direction on their US success.

"We would like to pass on our best wishes from all staff and students of Tong High School."

Getting to Number 1 in the US hadn't been easy—the boys had had to work so hard, squeezing in as many interviews and signings as possible in the run-up to the chart being announced. They'd literally not stopped; they just wanted to give it a final push. Naturally, they would have been a bit disappointed if the album had only got to Number 2, although it would still have been an amazing achievement for a UK act to make it into the Top 10 in US.

The first single the boys released was "What Makes You Beautiful"—a far stronger choice than doing a cover of "Forever Young," which would have been their first single, had they won *The X Factor*. It was released in the UK and Europe on September 11, 2011 but much later in the US—American fans had to wait until Valentine's Day 2012.

"What Makes You Beautiful" was also Number 1 in the US, Ireland, Mexico and the UK. A big hit worldwide, it ended up breaking lots of records, topping charts and going multi-platinum in many countries.

They filmed the video for "What Makes You Beautiful" in July 2011 on a beach in Malibu, California. It was directed by John Urbano, who would go on to direct a lot of the boys' future videos. Altogether it took them eighteen hours the first day and fourteen hours the next to film the three minutes twenty-seven seconds of footage. Harry tried to sunbathe when the cameras weren't rolling, and on one occasion he fell asleep. Zayn decided to sneak up on him and cover him with sand as a prank. Harry got a big surprise when he woke up!

John Urbano loved working with Harry, Niall, Liam, Louis and Zayn, and told the backstage cameras during filming, "The video's been going great, it's been a ton of fun. Working with the guys . . . they're amazing. They work so well with each other, you know, it's like they've been best friends forever and that's exactly what we're looking for."

The second single released in the UK and Ireland was "Gotta Be You" and it came out on November 11, 2011. The boys didn't have much chance to promote it, though, because they were really busy, but it still did well, peaking at Number 3. They had only filmed the video a month before in Plattsburgh at the State University of New York and at Lake Placid, New York. The story behind it is that the boys are leaving school and making their way to the lake to have a bonfire with some female friends. At the end of the video there is a fireworks display and Zayn walks towards a girl and kisses her.

Filming was eventful. Louis burned out the cooling system on the Mini Cooper he had to drive, Zayn crashed his moped and they all ended up going for a swim. They had found a small boat and decided to go out on the lake together, but Louis decided to have a laugh and throw Liam overboard. The other guys didn't want him to do it to them so they started wrestling, which caused the boat to capsize. They had to swim back to shore and were told off for fooling around and wasting the crew's time.

Zayn chatted to *Celebs on Sunday* magazine about what happened with the moped. He confided: "I smashed up a Vespa . . . I'm making this sound more glamorous than it actually was. It just span out and went crazy, ran on about two metres [about six-and-a-half feet] and hit some gravel. And it was a limited edition, worth thousands. They had to put red nail polish on it to cover the scratches."

Liam added: "He'd never driven a moped before and he had this brand new red one we were using in a video shoot—and crashed it."

The boys' second single to be released worldwide (and the third release in the UK and Ireland) was "One Thing." For this video they decided to stay in the UK and filmed in London as they traveled around in an open-top double-decker bus. Lots of fans turned up at Trafalgar Square to be part of the video after the boys tweeted to invite them and the bandmates were really grateful.

Filming took place on November 28, 2011, only weeks after the boys had filmed the video for "Gotta Be You" in

America but there was quite a gap before the single was available for purchase—it was on sale for digital download on January 6, 2012 in Austria, Denmark, Estonia, France, Germany, Greece, Hungary, Italy, Latvia, New Zealand, Poland, Portugal, Spain and Switzerland. On February 13, 2012, it was released in the UK and in America on May 22, 2012. It was Number 3 in Australia, Number 4 in Hungary, Number 6 in Ireland, Number 9 in the UK and Number 39 in America.

In April 2012 the bandmates did a mini-tour of New Zealand, performing in Auckland's Trusts Stadium and Wellington's St. James Theatre. When asked by TV3's *3 News* what he made of New Zealand in the short time they'd been there, Liam said: "Well, I've heard that it's the place where they invented the bungee jump, so I wanna try out where they invented the bungee jump."

Zayn wasn't up for it, though, because he has a fear of heights. In the end it was Liam and Louis who did the jump at the legendary Sky Tower, which is the tallest man-made structure in New Zealand. Heights isn't the only thing Zayn's afraid of, he confessed to Canada's *Vervegirl* magazine in March 2012: "I'm scared of a few things. I'm scared of heights. I don't like it when Louis messes about on the stairs, I hate it. I'm scared of rides. I'm also scared of water, I can't swim."

The final single from the *Up All Night* album was "More Than This," which was released in Australia, Ireland and the UK. The video was simply a recording of the boys performing the song and it premiered in Australia. Released for digital download in Australia on May 25 2012 and released in the UK and Ireland on June 26, 2012, it did best in Ireland, charting at Number 39. It was Number 49 in the Australian charts and Number 86 in the UK.

On Wednesday, August 1, 2012 the bandmates were presented with special plaques from their record company, as they had achieved 12 million sales in less than a year. It was an incredible achievement for the boys, who had worked so hard promoting *Up All Night* around the world.

Liam said at the time: "We are obviously ecstatic and incredibly humbled by our award. We have an incredible team of people around us who have helped us achieve this, and above all, we would like to thank our fans. We owe all our success to them."

Up All Night – Track by Track

Track 1 – "What Makes You Beautiful" – Written by Rami Yacoub, Carl Falk and Savan Kotecha. Produced by Rami Yacoub and Carl Falk.

Track 2 – "Gotta Be You" – Written by Steve Mac and August Rigo. Produced by Steve Mac.

Track 3 – "One Thing" – Written by Rami Yacoub, Carl Falk and Savan Kotecha. Produced by Rami Yacoub and Carl Falk.

Track 4 – "More Than This" – Written by Jamie Scott Produced by Brian Rawling and Paul Meehan.

Track 5 – "Up All Night" – Written by Savan Kotecha and Matt Squire. Produced by Matt Squire.

Track 6 – "I Wish" – Written by Rami Yacoub, Carl Falk and Savan Kotecha. Produced by Rami Yacoub and Carl Falk.

Track 7 – "Tell Me a Lie" – Written by Kelly Clarkson, Tom Meredith and Shep Solomon. Produced by Tom Meredith and Shep Solomon.

Track 8 – "Taken" – Written by Toby Gad, Lindy Robbins and 1D. Produced by Toby Gad.

Track 9 – "I Want" – Written by Tom Fletcher. Produced by Richard Stannard and Ash Howes\Track 10 – "Everything About You" – Written by Steven Robson, Wayne Hector and 1D. Produced by Steven Robson.

Track 11 – "Same Mistakes" – Written by Steven Robson, Wayne Hector and 1D. Produced by Steven Robson.

Track 12 – "Save You Tonight" –Written by RedOne, BeatGeek, Jimmy Joker, Teddy Sky, Achraf Jannusi, Alaina Beaton and Savan Kotecha. Produced by RedOne, BeatGeek and Jimmy Joker.

Track 13 – "Stole My Heart" – Written by Jamie Scott and Paul Meehan. Produced by Brian Rawling and Paul Meehan.

Track 14 – "Stand Up" – Written by Roy Stride and Josh Wilkinson. Produced by Richard Stannard.

Track 15 – "Moments" – Written by Ed Sheeran and Si Hulbert. Produced by Si Hulbert.

WHAT THE REVIEWERS THOUGHT:

In Billboard.com's review of the album, Jason Lipshutz wrote: "Let's get this right out of the way: first single 'What Makes You Beautiful' is the real deal. The song may not have earned its win over Adele's 'Someone Like You' at the BRIT Awards, but One Direction's smash hit is as endlessly playable as 'Bye Bye Bye' or 'Everybody (*Backstreet's Back*),' and as unstoppable as its 65 million Vevo views suggest. As the first song on *Up All Night*, 'What Makes You Beautiful' leads a front-loaded effort—its first three songs have doubled as its first three singles in the UK—that can make the debut album feel a bit top-heavy. Themes of innocent romance are constant throughout *Up All Night*, but tracks like 'Gotta Be You' and 'More Than This' hit a mark more smoothly than songs like 'Everything About You' and 'Taken.'

"Even on its weakest tracks, however, *Up All Night* demonstrates an originality in sound that was necessary for the revitalization of the boy band movement."

Hollywood Life were equally impressed, giving the album four out of five stars. In their review they stated: "Not since the golden age of boy bands in the mid-90s has a group emerged to convince me that the classic formula can still work—that is, until One Direction entered the picture. The British-Irish fivesome's debut album, *Up All Night*, is already burning up the US charts, and is it any wonder why?

"With catchy melodies, thoughtful lyrics, and more energy than a thousand Justin Bieber fans in a tiny box, *Up All*

Night feels like summer and Christmas and my birthday all rolled into one. In short, it just makes us happy."

Digital Spy reviewer Robert Copsey thought 1D delivered just what their fans wanted, writing: "Lead single 'What Makes You Beautiful'—a toe-tapping, Pink-meets-McFly mash up with a breezy guitar pop melody—sets the tone to a tee; with the lion's share of uptempos, including 'One Thing' and the title track, following a similar template. Fortunately, there's too much enthusiasm to accuse them of negligence.

"More surprising is their ability to carry off a sizeable ballad. The earworm chorus on 'More Than This' and heartfelt lyrics on 'Taken' ('You don't really want my heart/You just like to know you can') are some of the best slowies to come out of boyband land in recent years, making their decision to release the significantly less exciting 'Gotta Be You' as the second cut all the more mind-boggling. Sure, it's only playground love, but sometimes that's the best kind."

WHAT THE FANS THOUGHT:

Superfan Shelley was unable to choose her favorite track from the album, saying, "Obviously I love 'What Makes You Beautiful' (as do all Directioners!), but I love 'One Thing,' 'Stole My Heart' and 'Everything About You,' too.

"I really think that 'Some Mistakes' should have been their second song. Although 'Gotta Be You' is good, 'Some Mistakes' is even better! I think 'I Want' is so catchy, you can't help but sing along and I love the quirky melodies . . . it's brilliant.

"This really is an amazing album—there isn't a song on it that I don't love. There's a nice mix of songs, some to dance to and some to just wave your arms in the air and pretend you're at a concert, listening to them perform live!"

Nine-year-old Molly and Maisey couldn't agree on who has the best singing voice on the album (Molly loves Niall, while Maisey loves Zayn) but they could agree that "Little Things" is one of the best tracks. They say: " 'Little Things' is just such a wonderfully crafted song, and we love how the video was shot simply in black-and-white at a recording studio. 1D aren't just great singers, they are musicians, too and it was nice to see them playing guitars as well as singing.

"We also love 'Tell Me A Lie,' which is Zayn's favorite track from the album." In February 2013 'What Makes You Beautiful' was certified quadruple platinum by the Recording Industry Association of America (RIAA) after selling four million copies. For Zayn, getting to Number 1 in America was beyond anything he had ever hoped for. He would have been happy if One Direction were just popular in the UK, but to have hit singles in America and around the world was unbelievable.

In July 2012, he treated himself to a Bentley Continental GT car, costing a massive £32,000 ($48,681 dollars). Footballer David Beckham and rapper Nicki Minaj have the same car. It might seem very expensive to fans but it was a third of the price of Harry's Audi R8 Coupe.

Billboard's "21 under 21" list saw Justin Bieber pronounced the most powerful young music star in the world, but One Direction were in second place. What an achievement!

McFly's lead singer Tom Fletcher wrote the ninth track on the album, "I Want." Originally written for his sister Carrie, he decided to give it to Zayn and the boys to record for the *Up All Night* album. Fletcher enjoyed working with One Direction, telling *The Daily Star*: "They're a really likeable bunch of guys and they've got everything it takes to hit the big time." He enjoyed writing songs with them, as did his McFly bandmates, Danny Jones and Dougie Poynter. They worked hard, but played hard, too, playing FIFA football games and generally messing around.

Ed Sheeran wrote the track "Moments," which was one of the boys' favorite songs from the album. He had actually written it many years before but realized it was more suited to a group rather than something he should record himself. Sheeran explained to News.com how it had ended up on *Up All Night*: "I had a CD of forty songs I was giving to publishers. Harry was staying at my guitarist's friend's house at the time. They were putting their album together and they didn't have enough songs. I said, 'Here's a CD. If you want one of these songs, have it.' And it got on the album. It was a song I was never going to use. To have it on a multiplatinum selling album is quite nice."

The songs Zayn found hardest to perform on the album were "Save You Tonight" and "Tell Me A Lie" because he had to sing high.

Zayn has always loved performing but was less keen on the promotional side of being in a boy band—he has never been a fan of interviews. He would get really excited every time a new 1D tour was announced because performing for fans was something he loved to do. Of course the first tour the boys took part in was *The X Factor* Live Tour, which ran from February to April 2011. They got to sing "Only Girl," "Chasing Cars," "Kids In America," "My Life Would Suck Without You" and "Forever Young." Following this, they embarked on their first solo UK and Ireland tour, Up All Night, which began in December 2011 and ended in January 2012. During the course of the show they sang songs from their first album and five covers. Looking back, the boys admit their performance wasn't as polished as they might have liked and there were occasions when they sang out of tune or forgot their lines but that didn't happen very often and fortunately, the fans in the audience didn't judge them for it.

In February 2012 they were invited to support Big Time Rush at ten gigs in Canada and America. Although the band-mates had signed an American record deal just a few months earlier, this was a real privilege as they were virtually un-heard of in the States up until this point. Their record company decided to use social media to build a fan base and to get people talking about them in the US before their visit. "Twitter, Facebook and YouTube have been a large percent-age of the reason we've been known outside of the UK. We owe a massive thank you to the fans," Harry explained.

A website was set up (www.bring1dtous.com) and there was a competition for fans to win a visit from One Direction to their city. The website stated, "Are you ready to bring 1D to your city? Visit www.Bring1DtoUS.com now to get started on the first challenge. Click on your city for directions about how you can earn points for your city. Each challenge will bring you one step closer to a special 1D event in your city!"

The winning city was Dallas, Texas, and the boys arrived on March 24, 2012. Demand for wristbands for the event was so high that the venue had to be changed from Stonebriar Center Mall to the much bigger Dr. Pepper Ballpark, home to the Frisco RoughRiders baseball team. Fans could obtain a signed copy of *Up All Night* and watch One Direction perform.

On the day of their first show supporting Big Time Rush the boys were surprised to see people wearing One Direction T-shirts, holding up signs and singing along in the audience. At every single performance they received amazing support, which made Zayn and the other boys feel incredible. Already a fan of Big Time Rush, he used to watch their show on Nickelodeon so getting to tour with them was a surreal experience. Some fans didn't even stay to watch Big Time Rush perform, they just went outside to try and see One Direction before the bandmates headed back to their hotel.

The tour bus for the Big Time Rush tour was battered and the boys didn't keep it very clean. Many times the driver would have to pull over at fast-food restaurants because they were feeling hungry. They would order something and then take it back on the bus to eat. Sometimes they ended up having wrestling matches halfway through, so fries would end up everywhere.

When they performed in Toronto at The Air Canada Center Liam wore a Raptors basketball vest, as did Louis. Niall, Zayn and Harry wore blue-and-white Toronto Maple Leafs ice-hockey tops. An amazing night, it was one they would never forget. Just before their performance, the boys managed to lock their tour manager, Paul Higgins, in a toilet, something they found highly amusing!

After the boys performed in Nashville, they had to tidy their tour bus and then board a flight for New York at 5:00 a.m. They attended the *Big Time Movie* premiere and then the next day visited Z100, the biggest radio station in New York for an interview and to perform and meet some of their fans. When they performed on *The Today Show* a few days later, they had to be up at 5:00 a.m. again. It was their first interview on US television. The boys arrived on a big red bus and thousands of fans turned up to see them. They had literally become huge stars overnight.

The Up All Night Tour might have ended in January 2012 but it was extended to include Australia, New Zealand, America, Canada and Mexico. This leg of the tour started in April 2012 and ended on July 1, 2012.

Getting to visit other countries was a great bonus in the early days because as mentioned earlier, Zayn had never been abroad until *The X Factor*. The first time the boys went to Australia as a band, three hundred fans waited for them to arrive at Sydney Airport. It was so chaotic for their own safety they had to leave via a loading dock, which left the fans feeling terribly upset. The boys too felt awful and Niall tweeted, "Australia we're here, sorry we couldn't come out, airport police said it wasn't safe, we really wanted to come out and say hi, cya soon [sic]." They were taken to the InterContinental Hotel, where they would stay for the duration of their visit to Sydney. The boys had the penthouse suite right at the top of the building and much to the delight of fans below, Zayn appeared without a top on and Liam gave them a wave.

The bandmates enjoyed some time sunbathing on a yacht at Sydney Harbour and Zayn tried to sneak out with Louis to attend the premiere of Rihanna's movie *Battleship* without letting their security team know, but it didn't go as planned. Zayn explained to *The Sun*, "We did sneak away from our hotel at about 8:00 p.m.—it wasn't like it was three o'clock in the morning. But it was a bit like a smash-and-grab—we thought, let's go for it! Sadly, we didn't really know where we were going and we just kind of wandered around for a bit and got lost."

Being around the other boys 24/7 while touring proved intense and perhaps predictably at times there were arguments. When asked about their worst habits, the bandmates would say that Niall's was farting, Louis had smelly feet, Liam went to the gym the whole time, Zayn liked having the window down in the bus even when it was cold, while

Harry had two bad habits: snoring with his mouth open and stealing food from their plates.

Set list:
"Na Na Na"
"Stand Up"
"I Wish"
Medley: "I Gotta Feeling"/"Stereo Hearts"/"Valerie"/
"Torn"/"Moments"
"Gotta Be You"
"More Than This"
"Up All Night"
"Tell Me A Lie"
"Everything About You"
"Use Somebody"
"One Thing"
"Save You Tonight"
"What Makes You Beautiful"
Encore: "I Want"

For their UK and Ireland gigs (December 18, 2011–January 26, 2012) they were supported by Boyce Avenue and Matt Lonsdale, while in North America they were supported by Camryn, Manika and Olly Murs. In Australia they were supported by Justice Crew and Johnny Ruffo; in New Zealand, they were supported by Annah Mac. When their UK dates finished, the Boyce Avenue boys presented them with customized Baby Taylor guitars with "1D & BA" on the back and their autographs. An expensive gift,

Zayn started his career on *The X Factor* and loved performing on *The X Factor* Tour in February 2011.

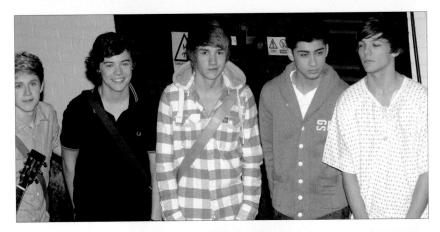

Above: Fresh-faced: One Direction have become used to photographers following them everywhere but it was all new when they left the *X Factor* Studios in November 2010.

Right: They have always been each other's biggest fans.

Left: Creating their own iconic Abbey Road shot.

Above: Trips back to Zayn's hometown of Bradford would never be the same again.

Below left: Zayn's fashion has changed significantly over the years, to say the least!

Below right: He always makes time for selfies with his fans.

Always on trend, Zayn has had many creative hair styles over the years.

Above: Forever excited to meet their fans, 1D at a meet and greet in Oxford Circus.

Left: Zayn looked drop dead gorgeous at the 2013 Teen Choice Awards.

The boys doing what they have done best over the years – performing.

Above: The boys show their fun side—covering the photographers with popcorn before the premiere of their movie, *This Is Us*.

Below: Raising money for charity has always been close to Zayn's heart. Here he is with a check with the other boys for $1,000,000 to help fight bullying.

Above: Zayn loved being at the Brits 2014, winning an award for best video and being honored with a special award for global success was something he'll never forget.

Below: Performing on *Good Morning America* in November 2013 was so much fun!

they would have cost Boyce Avenue a hefty £20,000 (about $31,000).

The boys liked to have fun while traveling from one concert venue to the next and enjoyed filming themselves doing weird dances to songs like Katy Perry's "Firework" and Carly Rae Jepsen's "Call Me Maybe." On the tour bus they played cards, watched movies, played on their PlayStations and chatted about all kinds of things. Sometimes they would run out of things to say so they would be silent for a while and they soon learned that it was important to sleep when they could. Being a twenty-first century singer means that every time you're not working, you're expected to update your social media accounts and interact with fans. Zayn and the other boys were expected to tweet quite a lot, but that didn't mean they couldn't also have fun and at times they would send the most obscure tweets to fans and answer their questions. In July 2011 one fan tweeted Zayn to ask: "What do you order at macdonalds[sic]? :')" to which Zayn replied: "2 fillet o fish burgers and a strawberry milkshake I'm not a fan of meals x."

By the time Zayn and the boys reached their hotel each night it would be very late, sometimes the early hours, and all they wanted to do was sleep. If fans were there waiting for them, Zayn would make an effort to pose for photos and have a chat because he was always grateful for their support. Sometimes he wanted to wind down after a show, other times he was keen to party. At times this would irritate the others— Liam would have to bang on his door at 1:00 a.m. to tell him to turn his music down.

Some nights it was hardly worth going to sleep for they would be woken at 5:00 or 6:00 a.m. by fans singing their songs outside. Even if they were ten floors up, they could still hear them singing because Directioners sing loud!

Zayn was thrilled when Olly Murs flew out to be their supporting act on the American leg of the tour. A runner-up on *The X Factor* in 2009, Murs had had several hit singles in the UK, including "Please Don't Let Me Go," "Thinking Of Me" and "Heart Skips A Beat." He became a really good friend of 1D during the six weeks he spent on the road with them and the Directioners really liked him, too, learning the words to his songs so they could sing along when he performed. Olly quickly became like an older brother to Zayn.

Olly told *USA Today* at the time: "The [One Direction] fans are insane! Running after the bus, jumping from trash cans, just so infatuated with the guys . . . One Direction fans wanted to know who I was. American fans are brilliant!"

In an interview with MTV, Olly said: "One Direction's fans, they literally found out I was supporting them. They went online, found out who I was, what songs I've done, my videos and then I walked out [at the] first gig in Detroit [and] everyone's just crazy.

"I was like, 'This is insane! They don't even know who I am. How could they be doing this?' "

In May 2012 the boys released the Up All Night Tour DVD, allowing fans who couldn't get tickets for the tour an opportunity to see the show. Having a copy of the show on DVD also meant that Zayn and the other boys had a lasting memento of their first real tour, something they could look back on. It went to Number 1 in an incredible twenty-five countries and sold over a million copies in the first three months of its release.

Before the release of the DVD the bandmates organized a special performance for some of their biggest fans in America. They were invited to a special screening of the DVD at an American diner, only for Zayn and the other boys to turn up, unannounced, and perform for them.

The girls were simply chatting to each other in the booths or on stools by the counter when, much to their surprise, Zayn, Louis, Liam, Niall and Harry suddenly appeared and started singing "What Makes You Beautiful" accompanied by an acoustic guitar. The girls were so happy!

Afterward, Harry admitted to the cameras: "I think when we play to, like, intimate crowds, I think a lot of our songs are really fun and kind of high energy, so when we do it acoustic, it's nice to kinda slow it down and have less people and just, you know, make it a little more personal and less about the atmosphere and more about the people in the room."

Niall added: "It's the people you get there—you get a natural reaction out of them because it's much more relaxed and, you know, they feel a bit more privileged or whatever to be in a smaller room with just us. So it's quite nice."

During the Up All Night Tour dates in America, Zayn would ride a miniscooter from the boys' dressing room to the canteen. On tour, the boys always had lots of gadgets and other things to play with, including quad bikes, go-karts and computer consoles with all the latest games to keep themselves entertained. They loved kicking a soccer ball around among themselves and the crew, so they made sure they took some soccer goals with them.

When the boys visited Niagara Falls on a rare day off they were driven in two police cars to a nearby arcade. A fan tried to break into one of the cars and got arrested.

Zayn enjoyed spending time on the 1D tour bus, telling Orlando radio station Mix105.1: "My best experience of touring is being on the tour bus—like, just chilling out . . . like, after the show, when you get off the stage and you're on the tour bus, chilling out, that's cool."

To combat boredom while traveling the boys loved playing pranks on each other. One day Harry shaved "HS" into Zayn's leg hair when he was asleep and Zayn shaved a slit into Liam's eyebrow. To prank Niall, Zayn decided to put lemon juice on his new trainers, which turned them yellow. Niall was so mad! While walking around (or onstage) the bandmates would sometimes pull each other's trousers down, which never failed to get a reaction. Arriving in Sweden, the other boys hid Zayn's luggage so he thought that he had left his things back in England.

It's impossible for Zayn to pick out just one favorite performance from the Up All Night Tour because there were so many memorable shows, but the last one at Fort Lauderdale, Florida, was pretty special for all the boys. Harry tweeted:

"Last show of the tour tonight. Thanks to an amazing crew, and everyone involved for making it what it was. Tonight will be fun." It was the end of an era as they had finished a run of over sixty shows worldwide. They had loved it but at the same time, they were desperate to have a break and go home to see their families. They had all had moments during the tour when they'd just needed a break to see their parents and siblings but they hadn't been able to stop, as their schedule was so packed.

Niall tweeted after the concert: "Wow ft,lauderdale! Great way to finish our 1st headline US tour! #upallnight tour is done! Long six months but amazing! Thank you all so much."

One of Zayn's favorite UK concerts was their final night in London on January 22, 2012. He tweeted: "London!! Smashed it amazing show thank you directioners never fail to impress me with their lung capacity u guys can scream! #amazingfans!"

Niall told his followers: "London incredible tonight! Off t chill now! Cant wait t sleep."

Harry summed up how they were all feeling when he told the backstage cameras, "I think for us the highlights of the tour have been the audiences. The audiences have been just so enthusiastic and really got involved so it's been good that they've been a part of the whole show, the whole experience."

When Harry turned eighteen, the boys were in LA so Zayn, Niall, Liam and Louis decided to play a prank on him. They were staying at the luxurious W Los Angeles – West Beverly Hills Hotel and booked Harry for a massage. He was finding it all very relaxing until the other boys came in halfway through and threw ice water over him!

The best prank Zayn ever played was when he and Louis managed to convince Harry, Niall and Liam that an actress pretending to be a Nickelodeon producer was about to give birth. They were sitting together on couches in the TV studio and the woman asked them all to sing to the baby because that would stop it kicking on her bladder so much. The boys started to sing "Rock-a-bye Baby" but then the actress began making noises and asked them to help because the baby was coming. Louis's mom was a nurse, so he went out to ring her for advice on what they should do, while the other boys tried to help the woman to her feet. Harry was the most shocked and tried to help the apparent mother-to-be in any way he could, telling Niall to go and get people to help. He had no idea that they were secretly being filmed with hidden cameras.

Poor Liam tried to speak to the woman's husband on her phone to let him know what was going on, but he was cut off. Meanwhile, Harry was trying to get her to breathe slowly. He couldn't help but snigger when Louis said it smelled, after which the woman admitted to having passed wind. Harry was very shocked when she informed them: "You've all been pranked by Nickelodeon." Zayn and Louis were so happy that they had managed to prank the others; they gave each other a hug and laughed at Harry's expense.

If you haven't see the video clip for yourself, make sure you check it out on YouTube; it's hilarious!

CHAPTER SIX

FINDING HOME

When Zayn first left the *X Factor* house he and the other boys moved into a hotel but on returning to London after the Christmas break, they were transferred to a luxury apartment, paid for by their record company in January 2011. All five of them lived together in the beginning but after a while Harry and Louis shared one apartment and the others had an apartment each.

The apartment complex was in Friern Barnet, North London. Previously Colney Hatch Lunatic Asylum in the Victorian era, it was a hospital for mental patients until 1993. It had been converted into luxury apartments, which then cost from around £500,000 (about $720,000) to buy. Former and current residents include Girls Aloud,

JLS, The Wanted, The Saturdays, Tulisa Contostavlos and England footballers Ashley Cole and Jermaine Pennant. The complex has a tennis court, gym, swimming pool and great security to prevent any fans from trying to sneak inside the gated community.

In 2012 the boys started moving out and buying their own houses in London. Zayn chose a £2 million ($3.2 million) five-bedroom house, which was really close to the one that Harry bought for £3 million ($4.8 million).

Before he moved in, Zayn told *The Sun*: "I have no furniture to fill the house but I'll give it a good go.

"It's really nice for me because growing up, we never really owned our own house—we always lived in a rented property. I don't come from a lot of money so for me to have my own house is a big achievement. That's all I ever wanted to do."

A few weeks later *Now Magazine* reported: "A team of removal men were spotted moving some of the nineteen-year-old One Direction singer's possessions into the property earlier this week. These included his blue motorcycle and two life-sized models, which bizarrely appeared to be of himself. One of the heavy mannequins was clad in a leather jacket and trilby hat while the other wore a white suit and one red glove. Zayn's new house boasts a number of impressive features, including a wine cellar, underfloor heating, a steam room, Jacuzzi and roof deck. The property's flat roof, large windows and unusual chrome doors give it a unique space-age look."

The Sun reported that Zayn's new home had a panic room so that he could hide if anyone ever broke into the property. They said it was also fitted with bulletproof doors, high-tech monitors and reinforced walls.

Zayn didn't just want to have a nice house for himself, though, he wanted to treat his whole family so he bought them a luxury home in Bradford. He told *Parade* magazine: "Now that we have a bit of money, it is nice to get gifts for people. Before I was getting and not really giving."

The moment when his mom and sisters received the keys to their new home was shown in the trailer of the One Direction movie, *This Is Us* (2013). Trisha was crying tears of happiness and called her "sunshine" to tell him how grateful she was. She said: "I know that you always used to say, "I'll get you a house one day when I'm older." But thank you for what you've done for us—I'm so proud of you."

An emotional Zayn replied: "Well, get off the phone then before I start crying."

In fact, Zayn was always the member of 1D who struggled most with fame. If he hadn't been a singer, he would have quite liked to become an actor. Before The X Factor he thought he would go on to university to study English and become an English teacher. When the bandmates enjoyed early success he was particularly concerned for Harry's well-being because he got the most criticism from the press and in the forums in the early days. In October 2012, Zayn told the Mirror "He is the baby of the group but people seem to forget that because of the way that he is and that he is so charming.

"So it is a little bit upsetting sometimes if you see him with the weight of the world on his shoulders. It does annoy us a bit. He's a young kid and people are just giving him grief for no reason."

CHAPTER SEVEN

GIRLS

Zayn used to say that he wished joining 1D hadn't made him more appealing to girls and that he'd always been as popular with the fair sex but he couldn't say that because it wouldn't be true. That said, he always had admirers in school—it's just that being in the band gave him millions of them!

Zayn was eight years old when he wrote his first love letter. He can still remember the first girl he gave a Valentine's card to, but he won't reveal her name. There was a special Valentine's mailbox at his school so he put his card in there and then it was delivered to her in class. He had his first kiss when he was nine or ten with a girl called Sophie Kirk and told *Heat* magazine: "She was one of triplets and I kind of dated all three of them." She was taller than Zayn and he couldn't reach so he needed to stand on a brick to be tall enough to lock lips with her! He thinks it was a bit like the Yellow Pages ad. But he didn't really like the kiss at all and found it embarrassing; he didn't want his family to find out he had kissed a girl either.

Zayn started liking girls when he was in high school and he had his first proper girlfriend when he was fifteen. They dated for nine months before splitting up. Zayn hasn't been out with many people and has only had about three serious relationships in his whole life. He has said he never lies about former girlfriends or past relationships, telling *Top of the Pops* magazine: "I've always been honest about that. What's the point of lying? You'll just get found out and then you'll look an idiot."

As a child, Zayn's dad Yaser was his hairdresser and then later when he was at school Zayn went through a phase where he wore a lot of hoodies and had a shaved head—he thought it made him look cool. In his early One Direction days he liked having his hair longer and fans loved his *quiff*. Every now and then, though, he wanted a change and in June 2012 he almost decided to shave his hair off until fans on Twitter convinced him otherwise. For the Olympics in 2012, he had an Elvis-inspired haircut with a blond streak, but by January 2013 the blond was gone and he was sporting a shaggy style. He went short again in the August before growing his hair slightly longer and adding a matching beard! By December 2013 his beard was less prominent and he had a subtle Mohawk. For most of 2014 he wore his hair long, in a shaggy mop. In January 2015, he sported a man bun with shaved sides. This new look was debuted in a photo shared by producer Naughty Boy (real name Shahid Khan) of Zayn in the studio with his team and "Read All About It" singer-songwriter Emeli Sandé. Zayn has never been afraid to experiment with his hair and goes for styles he likes at the time, rather than feeling restricted to those his fans will love.

What's more, Zayn has always said he cares more about a girl's personality than her looks, although he admits to being quite shallow when he was younger. When he was dating, he liked intelligent girls with amazing smiles and he has always thought you can tell a lot from a girl's eyes. He was never keen on girls who play mind games and prefers it when they are honest—he doesn't like girls who say one thing and mean something else. His favorite pick-up line was "Vas happening?" (What's happening?)

Zayn always said his ideal date would be going out for a meal and to watch a movie at the cinema and then returning home to "chill" with some drinks. Before dating his fiancée Perrie Edwards, his celebrity crushes were Megan Fox and Jessica Alba.

While living in the *X Factor* house the press linked Zayn to his fellow contestant Cher Lloyd, who went on to have a successful music career herself in both the UK and America. Cher decided to set the record straight and said in one of her video diaries for the show: "You asked if I was going out with Zayn . . . I'm not! He came in this morning in a green [onesie] . . . A green [onesie]! I don't think so, I really don't think so. Not cool!"

Once the competition was over, Zayn did end up dating one of the hopefuls, though. While they were taking part in The X Factor Live Tour he started to date Rebecca Ferguson, who had finished in second place. There was a six-year age gap and the press loved gossiping about them because Rebecca has two children, too. Rebecca told the *Mirror*: "I was with him for three months and people put so much focus on it because we were in the public eye.

"I was twenty-four then and I'd had two kids and other relationships so remember I'd had a lot of life experience before that. He's a footnote in my life maybe."

Zayn told *new!* magazine: "It shouldn't have happened. It was just a wrong idea from the start.

"It did end quite badly so we don't talk any more. We're not in touch at all."

In April 2012, Zayn went public about his relationship with Perrie Edwards from the girl group, Little Mix. Both tweeted after going on a date to the movies. Perrie wrote: "Just went to see avengers assemble and it was #boring. Good night though! xD @zaynmalik."

He replied: "@PerrieLittleMix yeah tonight was fun lets do it again sometime ;) x x."

Perrie's group, Little Mix, won *The X Factor* in 2011 after beating solo artists Marcus Collins and Amelia Lily. During the competition Zayn had admitted in an interview that he fancied the Little Mix girls, but he had no idea back then that he would end up dating one of them! It must have been helpful for him that Perrie understood what it was like to be on *The X Factor* and having to deal with instant fame. Before the pair started dating, he asked if she was up for having a relationship in the spotlight because girlfriends of the other boys had suffered abuse.

Only weeks after their first date some 1D fans began bombarding Perrie with vile tweets and even threatened to kill her. The situation became really unpleasant and true 1D fans were horrified by what was going on. Perrie ended up having to delete her Twitter account for a while just to stop the messages; the whole thing left Zayn feeling very angry and upset.

Despite the hassle Perrie received on Twitter she continued to date Zayn and in May 2012 told *This Morning*: "Obviously, we are together and everyone knows that now. I'm really, really happy." She was thankful that a lot of One Direction fans are also Little Mix fans and believed having to deal with the unkind tweets just meant she and Zayn had to toughen up. Perrie also told *Twist* magazine that Zayn was a much better boyfriend than some of the other men she had dated: "I'd been on a few dates in the past with other boyfriends that didn't go too well—I'd had loads of dating disasters! Zayn would never leave me with the bill, like the other boys used to do!"

Throughout their relationship some girls claimed that Zayn had asked for their number or cheated on Perrie with them, but he insisted it was all lies. They just wanted to make some money selling their stories and split Zayn and Perrie up. For a while Zayn ended up following Perrie's lead and deleted his Twitter account, telling followers: "Don't worry about me, im fine. I just deleted my account because of all the hate i was getting just by tweeting something simple. And all the rumors of me smoking weed and cheating. I dont need to read any of that negativity." He also said that he was sick and tired of seeing his mom and Perrie upset by the nasty comments. But the rumors didn't split Zayn and Perrie up and he even helped her get over a bad bout of tonsillitis in December 2012.

Perrie enjoyed doing the same things as Zayn and admitted to *Look* magazine: "We just chill out on the sofa. I'll wear the purple onesie Zayn bought me—he's got one, too!

"Everything's amazing . . . as long as we can talk as much as possible, we cope fine with being apart. The girls always say he's so good to me."

Zayn declared his love for Perrie during a Little Mix concert in Liverpool in February 2013, screaming, "Love you, Perrie! Love you, Little Mix!" His mom, Trisha, has been to see lots of Little Mix concerts, too and gets on really well with Perrie's mom, Debbie. Zayn also gets on well with Debbie and when he wanted a blond streak in his hair, he got her to do it, as he explained on the Irish TV Special, *The Story So Far*: "I probably should have passed it with someone, but I didn't—I just cut it. I was sat at home and just decided I wanted a bit of a blond streak. My girlfriend's mum did it for me. She's a hairdresser, so it was cool."

Perrie told the *Mirror* back in March 2013: "Zayn is my best friend and I've seen more of him since we finished our tour but it's hard as One Direction have been on tour as well.

"But we went to The BRITs together last month and had a great time."

When Zayn was in One Direction both he and Perrie did their best to ignore the negative stories in the press. They tried not to let the lies get to them, looked forward to the next time they would see each other and simply focused on having fun.

In May 2013, Perrie decided to play a prank on Zayn while he was sleeping and she gave him a manicure. She took a photo and posted it on Twitter—in the picture poor Zayn is fast asleep with a fedora hat covering his eyes and Perrie is holding up his hand to the camera to show off his nails. She tweeted: "The perks of your boyfriend not waking up through anything. Pretty LM nails Zayn (;"

After they got together Zayn and Perrie would speak to each other online and over the phone for hours each day. The pair quickly became the best of friends, as well as boyfriend and girlfriend, and could tell each other anything. Both come from loving, supportive families who are behind them 110 percent and want them to stay together, despite the negative stories in the press. Zayn found that he enjoyed spending time with Perrie's family when he wasn't working; he would accompany them to her concerts and cheer her on from the sidelines. Being quite a shy person, he was somewhat apprehensive the first time he met them. He told James Robertson from the *Mirror* in October 2012: "I went up to meet her mum and family the other month. I was a bit scared of meeting her brother, to be honest—he's in the navy, he's a big bloke.

"I thought he was going to be a bit defensive over his sister but he was cool."

In an interview Zayn's mom, Trisha, did with *Heat* magazine when she went to see Little Mix perform on *The X Factor*, she said: "She would be a perfect daughter-in-law. I don't think we'll be seeing a proposal anytime soon, because they both want to focus on their careers.

"She's lovely, though. Zayn saw her on the telly and knew he liked her—he just had to convince her. Our families are each other's families now."

In fact, at the time, Zayn openly admitted in several One Direction interviews that he wanted to be married by the time he turned thirty. He is very close to his mom—he loves her so much and always wants her to be happy. Trisha is not at all controlling and she told the *Mirror* before he got engaged to Perrie: "Fans ask me for permission to marry him but he can choose his own Mrs.

"When he leaves home I cry at the gate and he says, 'Mum! I'm not going to war!' A driver comes for him and I have to stand there and wave back at him. I go to London a lot and do all his washing. I don't expect Zayn to text me all the time, but I text him 'Night, night, son' and he texts back, 'Love you, Mum.' "

When Harry, Liam, Louis, Niall and Zayn were interviewed by MTV in October 2012 they were asked who they thought would be the first of the boys to walk down the aisle. Harry believed it would be Liam (he was dating Danielle Peazer at the time), but Liam thought that Zayn was the most likely bandmate. He thought he would do it on the spur of the moment, while Niall predicted that Zayn would get married in Las Vegas.

There was further speculation as to whether "Zerrie" would be the first to tie the knot after Zayn got a tattoo of Perrie on his upper arm in June 2013. Based on a sketch that he had done, it is a cartoon of Perrie wearing a bobble hat and CND T-shirt. He had it done while the boys were in Maryland. At first Perrie was shocked because she had no idea that Zayn had been planning to get a tattoo, but when she saw it she liked it. He later added a large pair of angel wings in black-and-white to his chest and some red lips, which people believe are shout-outs to Perrie.

Perrie became a huge fan of Zayn's tattoos, which was a good thing because he is constantly adding to his collection (47 in total at last count). But he doesn't get tattoos to make a statement or to show off, he gets them to remind himself of special people and special moments in his life. He got his Zap tattoo because he loves comics and for no other deep reason (some fans wrongly believed that he had his Zap tattoo because it stands for Zayn and Perrie). Of course he knows it's geeky, but Zayn was really into collecting comic books when he was younger.

Zayn has lost count of the number of tattoos he has. He told Capital: "I haven't got much space left on my body. I just got a tattoo on my leg and my arm. I did them both in the same session. I got a tattoo of the name of the album and I got something on my leg, it's kinda of weird. It's just an outline of a dude smoking."

On his stomach he has a pack of cards with a crown and his initials on it, with the phrase "It's a pirate's life for me" below, while "be true to who you are" in Arabic appears on his left collarbone. He added the word "FRidAY" next to it, which was an in-joke with the other members of 1D, as Zayn always used to ask, "Is it Friday yet?" Walter (his grandad's name) appears on his chest in Arabic, he has the yin and yang symbol on his wrist and a Japanese symbol on his hip, which means "born lucky." He has a large gun tattoo in black-and-white on his hip and a geometric tattoo of two circles, a square and a circle and a lightning bolt tattooed on the back of his right arm. The crown tattoo on his chest stands for his last name "Malik," which, as we already know, means "king."

On his right forearm he has a "fingers crossed" tattoo, about which Zayn told *Seventeen* magazine, "It's for the future—a hope that everything goes well." He has a life-size microphone tattoo on his right forearm, which he had done because singing and performing is so important to him, and always will be. Underneath the microphone is an ink splatter tattoo and on the back of his arm is a large boombox. Next to this is a bandana tattoo, which sits on his elbow, and he also has the word "chillin" in bubble letters next to a palm tree.

Zayn has a detailed henna-style black-and-white flower above his left wrist, which joins with a Hindu mandala tattoo on his hand. On his lower stomach he used to have the Chinese symbol for "born lucky" but had it changed to a heart. He has a silver fern on the back of his neck—a New Zealand symbol for good luck—and a jigsaw piece near his elbow; he has quite a few number tattoos, too. At first fans didn't understand the significance of the numbers but then they realized that together they formed Zayn's *X Factor* number: 1-6-5-6-1-6.

And Zayn has several animal tattoos—a wolf, bird, tiger, snake and monkey (wearing a spacesuit). He has BUS 1 tattooed on the outside of his left hand, which is rumored to be a shout-out to one of 1D's tour buses, and a Pink Floyd Prism-inspired tattoo on his right bicep to match a tattoo that Harry has (in fact, Zayn held his friend's hand when Harry had his first tattoo, a star, done by LA tattoo artist Freddy Negrete). He has a fondness for skulls and has a smoking skull in a top hat on his left shoulder, a skull and crossbones on his right shoulder and a large skull with a slingshot on his right arm.

Zayn was so excited about the prospect of 1D's Madison Square Garden concert in 2012 that he had "M.S.G." with the date "3 12 12" added to his arm by tattooist John Bahel. Louis also decided to have the same tattoo, so he too would have a lasting memento. It was a legendary venue, and they'd managed to sell more than 20,000 tickets in less than a minute!

All the 1D boys decided to have matching tiny screw tattoos on their ankles in 2012, although Niall took some convincing. He hates needles so getting a tattoo isn't his idea of fun! The boys chose screws to remind themselves to stay grounded, no matter what.

Trisha and the other 1D moms hoped the boys wouldn't get too many tattoos but at one stage they seemed to be adding to their collections every few months. During an interview with *Daybreak* in January 2013, Liam admitted: "My mum went crazy about the whole tattoo idea."

Zayn added: "Simon [Cowell] hasn't said anything but our mums have been like, "Maybe you're getting a bit too much.' "

In a separate interview with *Top of the Pops* a year later Zayn confessed: "Obviously, mums don't really like tattoos, and she's a bit like, "When you're older, what are you going to do?' But I think when I'm an older bloke, they'll still look cool."

Zayn used to say he was the bad boy of One Direction but he thought that he was misunderstood a lot of the time. He has openly admitted to being addicted to tattoos and who knows how many tattoos he will end up with as he has so many already? He told *Now* magazine: "I want to fill my entire arm up to my elbow to start. I've got loads of ideas. I draw as well. I'm more addicted to coming up with the ideas of what I can get tattooed rather than the actual tattoo itself."

He also revealed that Perrie was a fan, saying: "Oh yeah! She likes my tats. She's into the whole rock 'n' roll look." At the *This Is Us* premiere in London on August 20, 2013 it was revealed that Zayn and Perrie were indeed engaged, as Perrie was wearing a three-stone diamond ring on her ring finger. A few days later, Zayn admitted on *The Today Show*: "There's not much to say . . . we are engaged, really happy."

Perrie's mom Debbie told her local newspaper, the Dorset Echo "It's official. I'm over the moon. They are really in love . . . It's wonderful because Zayn is absolutely gorgeous. It's true they got engaged on Sunday and it's absolutely lovely. Perrie loves him to pieces and it's perfect. They get on so well together and understand each other. It's just fabulous."

In a separate interview with Real Radio she revealed: "He did the traditional asking me and then asking his mum and dad and everything. It was fabulous—just lovely."

When asked how long it would be until the pair would walk down the aisle, Debbie said: "I mean, obviously they've got so much to do . . . they'll wait till 2014, 2015 . . . One Direction are doing so much and Little Mix are the same. They're out of the country most of the time doing their promotion for this, that and the other, so it's just unbelievable. But I think they will eventually get together and set the date."

CHAPTER EIGHT

FAN LOVE

Zayn used to say that there were three types of One Direction fans—those who scream, the ones who want to talk to them and those who don't say a word. Over the years of being in the band he witnessed quite a few fans fainting in front of him because they were just so overwhelmed at meeting him and the rest of the boys. This used to scare him initially but he soon got used to it. He told *We Love Pop* magazine in May 2012 about one particular incident: "Obviously you don't get to see things like that unless you are the Beatles, who have that power, and to see it that close was a bit scary. I didn't really enjoy her fainting in front of me, however, it was cool to know I could make a girl faint!"

In June 2012, Zayn sprained his wrist so he had to wear a bandage during 1D's performance in Las Vegas. Soon the hashtag #GetWellSoonZayn was trending on Twitter. Zayn was very touched by this. He has always been overwhelmed by the kind messages fans send him and admits that he considers his fans to be part of his extended family.

Zayn genuinely cares about all his fans and appreciates every card, letter, drawing and present he has been sent over the years. He was so grateful to the people who picked up their phones and voted for One Direction in every week of the *X Factor* live shows because without their support the boys wouldn't have made the final or secured a record deal afterward.

Zayn has always insisted that he doesn't want fans spending lots of money on presents but he appreciates everything he receives, whether it's a pack of Skittles, a notepad or a T-shirt. If you're a budding artist, why not send him a sketch or two.

The best present Zayn ever received from a fan was a birthday cake from a four-year-old for his nineteenth birthday. He was chilling at home with his family when he heard a knock at the door and when he opened it, she was standing there, holding the cake. He might have received some amazing cakes on his birthdays since then (courtesy of Perrie), but he will never forget how excited the little fan was to meet him that day.

Zayn has fans of all ages, the oldest one being ninety-nine-year-old Jenny Gasston, Perrie's grandmother. He met her for the first time on May 18, 2014 when he turned up, unannounced, at her home in South Shields, near

Newcastle. Perrie had performed with Little Mix the night before at the Metro Radio Arena, Newcastle, so she used the opportunity to catch up with her family.

Her gran told the *Daily Mail*: "Zayn is absolutely lovely. It's the first time I've met him and I was thrilled we could meet. He was very nice. We had a nice cup of tea and some sponge cake and he could also see Perrie, which was nice.

"Meeting him for the first time went very well. It was a pleasure to meet him. I love One Direction—my favorite song is 'Little Things.' I have got all their CDs but I didn't have them with me for Zayn to sign.

"Him and Perrie are lovely together and I wish them all the luck in the future."

Perrie's Uncle Stuart added: "Little Mix are doing their arena tour and Zayn and One Direction are doing their stadium tour. Obviously this means that at the moment they don't really get to spend much time together.

"My mother was [at the house] and she is their oldest fan. She loves Little Mix and she thinks that Zayn is the best thing since sliced bread. It's the first time she met Zayn and she was so thrilled. Unfortunately, she is slightly losing her sight so when Zayn first walked in she didn't realize it was him to begin with.

"He was absolutely wonderful with her. We had to take plenty of pictures. He put his arm around her and everything. It was really nice for the kids to get together, too. They don't get to see enough of each other, if you ask me." When Zayn was in 1D he was always surprised at the lengths some fans would go to meet him and the rest of the boys. He saw them hide in garbage cans, pretend to work in the hotels where they were staying and chase down their van in busy traffic. While out and about he loved meeting fans but always warned them not to risk their own safety to see him—running down a busy street is never a good idea!

One of Zayn and Liam's scariest encounters with a fan happened in the early days with One Direction when they were at Heathrow Airport. They confessed all to Maude Apatow from *Teen Vogue* magazine in February 2012.

Liam revealed: "We were in Heathrow once and there were about five hundred girls at the airport. We went out the side door to try to get to our car but we couldn't get to it. Zayn's hoodie got ripped off. I got a good whack in the face." Zayn added: "There was a security booth outside and it was all glass. People were licking the windows. It felt like we were in a zombie movie."

If someone asked Zayn how many interviews he did while he was in One Direction he wouldn't have been able to say—it was literally thousands. On some days he could do more than twenty interviews with journalists and this was understandably draining for him and the other boys. Sometimes they would only be in a country for a day before moving on so Zayn soon got used to sleeping whenever he could. The boys' schedule was so packed that it was unusual for them to get a few days off in a row.

Because they had to do so many interviews it was extremely rare for them to be asked something unique and often journalists would pose the same questions again and again, questions any fan would already know the answer to. This was frustrating for the boys because it was hard not to give the same reply again and they also knew that fans would be bored when they read or watched the interview because it wasn't telling them something new. Zayn much preferred it when journalists asked their fans to tweet in questions they wanted answered because it meant they would be asked something different from the norm.

During one Canadian interview in October 2012, the radio host DJ Rush from *The Morning Hot Tub* refused to talk to Zayn because he'd been given a list of questions and topics he couldn't discuss with Zayn by a member of One Direction's press team. The banned questions were:

1. What is your celebrity crush?
2. Which of you have girlfriends?
3. Who came up with the name One Direction?
4. Anything *X-Factor* related
5. Worst habits about each other
6. Do you guys fight?
7. Best prank someone played on you
8. Describe each other in one word
9. Funniest fan stories
10. If not in the band, what would you be doing?
11. Pre-show rituals
12. Anything about money or religion

These were all questions that fans already knew the answers to so it's understandable that he was requested by 1D's management team not to ask them again. They weren't being difficult, they were just trying to encourage the radio host think of some fresh and new questions to ask. However, DJ Rush was angry that he had been given the list and decided to show this once he was on the phone with Zayn. He said: "Hi Zayn, you're a very busy guy. I want to talk to you but I can't do that . . . no *X Factor*, no pranks . . . Well, that's about going to do it. Thanks for taking the time to talk to us and continued success for the future." Then he hung up on him without asking a single question. It was a strange reaction, as lots of One Direction fans had been looking forward to hearing the interview.

A recording of the phone call quickly went viral but rather than criticizing the radio host, the media decided to criticize Zayn instead and he received a barrage of abuse. He explained to Scott Mills on BBC Radio 1 in a later interview: "The reason she [the press team member] was saying you can't ask these questions is because of the fans.

"They want to hear some new things; they want to know what's going on. They don't want to hear the same things over and over again. We always get asked the same questions so we just thought we'd mix it up a bit and try and rule out a few questions so we get some new ones."

Zayn never wanted to be false with his fans and was always keen to give honest answers in interviews: he wanted them to understand what made him tick. When he learned that a 3D documentary movie titled *This Is Us* was to be released in August 2013, he was delighted. He wanted fans to be able to see what it was like to be in One Direction, to catch a glimpse of the boys' lives behind the scenes as they traveled the world. As he explained to *Heat* magazine in February 2013: "It's just going to be the stuff you don't get to see—the day-to-day waking up in the morning, actually traveling."

The movie's director was the American independent filmmaker Morgan Spurlock, who up until this point had been most famous for his documentary movie, *Super Size Me* (2004), which saw him eat three McDonald's meals a day for thirty days to study the effect it had on his body. Spurlock was thrilled to be chosen, telling the press in November 2012: "This is an incredible opportunity and an amazing moment in time for the band. To capture this journey and share it with audiences around the world will be an epic undertaking that I am proud to be a part of."

Simon Cowell added: "I'm delighted we're making this film and Morgan is the perfect person to give that access-all-areas, behind-the-scenes look into what it's like to be One Direction today. What the band have achieved is incredible. They and their fans have made history around the world—this is for them."

Filming started on January 17, 2013 when the boys were visiting Tokyo and they were filmed as they traveled to different countries over the following months. As well as containing footage from behind the scenes, and interviews with fans and those associated with the band, Spurlock used live footage taken from one of their concerts at The O2 Arena in London. To get them involved, fans were encouraged to send in self-portrait photos to appear in the background of the poster for the movie. Thousands of photos were used but it was difficult for the fans to spot themselves and many felt disappointed that they hadn't been chosen. To combat this a second poster using more fan photos was designed and appeared on the official 1D website with an app that fans could use to try and pinpoint their own photo.

When the trailer for the movie was released in June 2013 it contained a snippet of the boys' track "Best Song Ever," which was from their third album, *Midnight Memories*. This built excitement and thousands of fans rushed to midnight showings on the movie's release on August 29.

This Is Us proved a smash hit at the box office, making almost £3.5 million in the UK alone on its opening weekend, and $17 million in the US. The boys were thrilled that it did so well, with Harry telling the press: "We made this for the fans. We just want to say a massive thank you to them."

The hype might have been huge but many older fans and critics alike were somewhat disappointed. They felt the movie was too polished and didn't show everything they would have liked to have seen, partly because it was rated PG but designed to be suitable for as young an audience as possible.

The Telegraph critic only managed to give it two out of five stars, saying, "*One Direction: This Is Us* is a straightforward account of the group's three-year rise to fame, culminating in two sold-out nights at the 50,000-capacity Foro Sol arena in Mexico City. Even readers who are unfamiliar with the work of Harry Styles, Zayn Malik et al. may still be aware that the five-piece was constructed during the seventh series of *The X Factor*: they finished in third place, but were signed to Simon Cowell's record label anyway. Cowell pops up towards the start of the film to marvel, with an admirably straight face, at their entirely organic rise to stardom."

Chris Tookey of the *Daily Mail* felt the movie was too safe, but still gave it three out of five stars. He wrote: "Director Morgan Spurlock made his name with a documentary *Super Size Me* that targeted the fast food industry. It's hard to avoid the conclusion he's sold out by making a movie eulogizing the fast music industry. This film is uncompromisingly upbeat and on message; no word of criticism of Cowell or the group is allowed on screen.

"But creatively Spurlock makes a good job of filming the group's O2 concert in 3D, and his fly-on-the-wall style of film-making captures the group's high spirits, natural good looks and sheer likeability in a way that's a good deal more attractive than similar attempts by others to capture the appeal of U2 and the Jonas Brothers."

Despite receiving mixed reviews the movie was a huge hit worldwide, with many Directioners going to see it multiple times. *This Is Us* earned $28,873,374 in North America alone, and $68,532,898 worldwide. It topped box offices in many countries and became the fourth biggest concert movie ever, with only *Justin Bieber: Never Say Never, Hannah Montana & Miley Cyrus: Best of Both Worlds* and *Michael Jackson's This Is It* doing better.

One Direction: This Is Us was released on DVD and Blu-ray, including bonus footage and interviews, in North America on December 17, 2013 and on December 19, in the UK. This too did incredibly well worldwide as many Directioners asked for it for Christmas! In the UK alone 270,000 copies were sold in the first three days of its release.

Of course the fans wanted a follow-up movie and were pleased when the boys announced that they were releasing *One Direction: Where We Are—The Concert Film* on October 11, 2014. This allowed those fans unable to get tickets to the tour to see the show and experience what they would have experienced, had they been in the audience. The concerts they chose to film took place at San Siro Stadium, Milan, Italy on June 28 and 29, 2014.

The movie was only in cinemas for two days and it broke "event" movie records, taking $15 million at the box office worldwide. It was the top trending topic on Twitter, with fans everywhere talking about how amazing Zayn and the other boys were, and how great the show was.

CHAPTER NINE

FAMILY TIME

You would struggle to find any musician as dedicated to his family as Zayn. Family will always be the most important thing in Zayn's life and he will always put them before anything else. Being in One Direction and traveling the world was extremely difficult for him because he missed his mom, dad and sisters so much. He admitted to *The Sun* in October 2012: "It's really been hard. Last weekend was the first time in six months that I've been home.

"I do feel like I've missed out a bit because I was really close with my sisters when I was at home. It must be weird for them but they cope really well."

Some of Zayn's favorite 1D performances were when his family came to see him. He told *Daybreak* in January 2013:

"It's really nice just to, like, look out [at the audience] and see your family, however embarrassing they're being.

"Even if they're on the chair dancing, like, it's just cool."

In 2013, Zayn's mom, Trisha, won an Inspirational Mom award from her local council because of the way she has raised her children and the fact that she is an inspiration to other mothers in Bradford. Zayn was so happy when he found out she had won. On the competition website there is an interview with Trisha. In it, she says: "As a child I grew up in a very close-knit family. Born in a traditional white British working-class family, and as I grew up, I married a lovely British Pakistani man and became part of a loving British Muslim family. Coming from a completely different upbringing and background I have always tried to learn as much as I can about my husband's religion and culture, so that I can ensure my children maintain their British values and also learn about their father's roots and religious values. Integration and learning other languages and religion I must admit has been difficult, but I am happy to say I have a very happy family, both from my husband's side and from my family side.

"I have four children—three daughters aged twenty-one, fourteen and ten, and a son aged twenty. My son has recently achieved huge success within the music industry, yet I try my best to ensure my children continue to remain humble and remember their early years of growing up in East Bowling. I brought up my family with very little money, living in a rented property in East Bowling. I have been working at Lowerfields Primary School for the last three years as a Halal Chef and continue to do so, despite my son's superstar success. I have always allowed my children the complete freedom to follow whatever they feel comfortable with, however, I have also ensured that they have an understanding and knowledge of both mine and my husband's cultures and religions. As well as supporting my son with his music I have also made sure and encouraged his education at mosque and school. I continue to support my husband and family by working at a school and despite my family's new success, I remain local in Bradford. My son's success has changed things for me and my family, and it has become difficult for my family and I to try and maintain a normal life, however, the future of my children is important and I feel as a mother my role is more difficult now to ensure I maintain the stability they have grown up with and that I am always there for them to ensure they cope with the change that has entered their lives."

When Zayn was in One Direction, he might have been thousands of miles away from his family most of the time but he was always in cell phone contact and he knew that he could get in touch with them any time of day or night, although sometimes being in a different time zone made things difficult. His mom, Trisha, once admitted to the BBC: "He went to Australia recently and I didn't see him for almost three months. It's sad but the family had to check on the Internet to see where he was."

In August 2012, Zayn loved having the opportunity to take Perrie to Bradford to celebrate Eid with his family. Eid is a time when Muslims celebrate the end of Ramadan, which is the ninth month of the Islamic calendar, and when fasting is observed. A photo of them all together was shared on Twitter and although 1D fans sent lovely comments, they also received lots of abuse from racist trolls.

Upset by this, Zayn decided to delete his Twitter account for a time. He told the *Mirror*: "I believe that your religion should be between you and whoever your belief is in.

"I don't think you should stick it in people's faces. I think you should just keep it to yourself and that's how I've always been with it. I had just seen a few things that had annoyed me.

"I thought we had moved away from that and we're living in the 21st century and people could accept people from different religions. It shouldn't have wound me up, but it did."

But Zayn eventually decided to go back on Twitter, having thought of all the millions of fans who would be disappointed otherwise. As he explained: "There are so many fans on there who say nice things every day, so why should they miss out?"

It's not just Zayn who gets upset about the nasty things that are written about him. His mom told the BBC in December 2013: "Me and Zayn's dad stopped looking at social media because he [Yaser] used to get upset about what people had written.

"It's like a kick in the gut to read things that are, most of the time, not even true."

No matter where he is in the world, if there is a family emergency then Zayn will drop everything and fly home. In March 2012 his auntie died and he flew home as soon as he could to support his family and to attend her funeral. It meant that he missed some concerts in North America so the other 1D boys had to adapt the show to cover for him. Of course they completely understood why Zayn had to be with his family, though. Harry tweeted: "Zayn has suffered a loss in his family & has had to go home for a few days so won't be at our next shows in the US."

Zayn's family live relatively normal lives and his mom only gave up work at the end of 2013 at his insistence. Trisha explained to journalist Shabnam Mahmood: "Zayn said, 'You don't have to do this anymore.' Instead, he puts my wage into my bank.

"I still shop in my local supermarket and go to the discount store for a pair of shoes."

Trisha does occasionally get recognized when she goes shopping and she finds it funny when girls ask if they can have a photo taken with her. She told ITV News in March 2012: "The worst time for me is if I go to Zayn's tour. I do get stopped outside and they say, 'Can we have a photo with you?' It's quite flattering when people stop you and say, 'Can I have a photo with Zayn's mum or Zayn's sisters?' It's quite scary, really, sometimes. I think we were in Wolverhampton, and me and my daughter had to be removed from security because all the fans just stood up, and it was quite scary to think that you're going to get mobbed by all the fans. So we had to be removed and moved up to a balcony."

When Zayn was in 1D he used to get so excited when he got to go home to see his family in the early days that he'd occasionally tweet to tell his followers that he was Bradford-bound. Sometimes fans would turn up on Trisha's doorstep and leave him gifts or tie things to their gate. They never left too many items so it didn't impact the family too much. Trisha enjoyed chatting to the fans and finding out what songs they liked, and talking about Zayn. She really hoped that Zayn and Perrie will settle nearby someday, telling the BBC: "If they have children I wouldn't like to be so far away from them. I would really like to still be part of their lives."

CHAPTER TEN

FOOD, GLORIOUS FOOD

Zayn has always loved eating and he once said that if he could have dinner with anyone, alive or dead, it would be Michael Jackson. He is always up for trying something new or taking part in a food-related challenge. While living in the *X Factor* house, back in 2010, he took some cooking lessons and played up to the cameras, pretending to be a food expert while wearing a black wig, but he didn't take the lessons very seriously and instead messed around with Louis. He also took part in a "Chili Challenge" with his fellow *X Factor* contestants, Paije Richardson and John Adeleye. They had to eat four chilies and if they took a gulp of milk, they would be disqualified. John struggled with the second chili, while Paije had difficulties with the third, but all three managed to eat their four chilies without reaching for the milk! Zayn was by far the best, though, because he ate them as if they weren't hot at all.

In another challenge (called "Brain Freeze"), Zayn managed to beat Paije and Geneva from the girl group, Belle Amie. The challenge involved seeing how many ice cream shots they could take before experiencing "brain freeze." Geneva only managed two, but Paije and Zayn ended up tied, with four shots. To decide on a winner, both had to eat three ice cream shots without using their hands and the fastest person won. Zayn was the fastest, so he was declared the Brain Freeze champion!

While touring with One Direction, Zayn's food was prepared by chef Sarah Nicholas, who was in charge of making sure that the boys, their musicians and the crew ate a varied, healthy diet. She let them have their favorite meals regularly but she would cook healthier versions. Sarah was always impressed by how easy it was to cook for Zayn because he isn't a fussy eater and likes dishes such as Spaghetti Bolognese and spicy chicken (chicken is a particular favorite). She told the *Daily Star* in March 2013 that Louis's favorite food is Special K and that Niall likes "sausage and mash, pies, creamy chicken pasta or chicken Kiev," adding that Louis drinks the most tea and the boys "also drink more juices and water than fizzy drinks. Before they go onstage, they tend to have orange or apple juice, Capri-Suns or Rubicon."

If you want to see some examples of the type of things Sarah cooked for Zayn when he was touring with One

Direction, head to her website and check out the sample menus. Her website address is: www.sarahskitchentouring. com. She has cooked for comedian Peter Kay, Olly Murs, Il Divo, Elvis Costello, JLS, Will Young and many more stars.

Of course, Zayn and the other boys didn't just stick to the food Sarah prepared when they were on the road. They would also eat out and order takeout, asking their drivers to pull over to let them get food from service stations on long trips. When performing at Newcastle's Metro Radio Arena in April 2013, they ordered in the following dishes from Nando's (a popular South African restaurant chain that specializes in chicken dishes):

Zayn: 1 x double chicken pitta (medium) with cheese, 1 x mixed olives, 1 x coleslaw, 1 x corn on the cob, 1 x hot sauce, 1 x extra-hot sauce

Harry: 1 x double chicken (mango & lime) wrap with cheese and pineapple

Liam: Butterfly chicken (medium, no skin), mixed olives, 1 x Perinaise sauce

Louis: 1 x half chicken (medium), 1 x creamy mash, 1 x Perinaise sauce

Niall: 1 x double chicken wrap (medium, no lettuce), 1 x spicy rice, 5 x wings (medium), 1 x Perinaise, 1 x medium sauce

Sarah might be a great chef, but Zayn couldn't help but miss his mom Trisha's cooking when he was touring. He told *The Sun* magazine in July 2012: "I love samosas filled with mincemeat—my mum makes really great ones."

Niall loved her cooking, too, adding: "Zayn's mum makes such good food—I can eat so much!" Zayn used to say he was a little bit jealous of how Niall can eat anything without putting on weight, telling *Top of the Pops* magazine in May 2014: "Niall is the skinniest . . . he just eats and eats and eats and eats. But he never puts any weight on!

"It's a little bit annoying. The rest of us have to watch what we eat, but Niall can eat just anything and be fine."

CHAPTER ELEVEN

TAKE ME HOME

Zayn loved promoting *Up All Night*, but he loved going into the studio to record the boys' second album even more. There might have been pressure for them to record an even better album than the first, but he and the rest of the boys were more than up to it. They were looking forward to working again with Ed Sheeran and all the other amazing songwriters and producers they had worked with first time around. Now, however, they wanted *Take Me Home* to have more guitars than *Up All Night* because they had really enjoyed having guitars on their tour; they also wanted to write more themselves.

Zayn loved having the opportunity to work with Ed Sheeran and told Capital FM in October 2012: "It's all just chilled—the whole vibe of his studio is chilled out.

"He's got a field and sometimes you just sit out on the field and jam with a guitar, play a little bit of football, walk into the studio when you feel like it, walk back out when you feel like it. It's wicked!"

In the buildup to the album being released the boys' press team gave the following statement to the media: "The eagerly awaited second album is due for release in November 2012 and sees One Direction collaborating with a whole host of first-class writers and producers. As well as reuniting with the likes of Rami Yacoub & Carl Falk and Savan Kotecha, Ed Sheeran and McFly's Tom Fletcher, the album features input from Dr. Luke, Shellback and Toby Gad. The album is sure to be another huge smash release from a truly international pop phenomenon."

The songwriters and producers from the first album also worked on the second album, something the boys were pleased about because they got on so well with them and understood the kind of music the group wanted to make. Songwriter Savan Kotecha explained to Billboard.com why he thinks 1D have been successful in America, stating: "It felt like everyone tried to do boy bands by going to the cool, hip producers who were coming up.

"We wanted to make it very vanilla. You're aiming for teens and tweens with boy band guilty pleasure music. We weren't trying to be urban or rhythmic, and they happened to share the same vision."

The boys loved having the opportunity to write tracks with some of the best songwriters and producers in the world. Liam explained to Billboard.com how the writing process worked. He said: "It was actually usually groups of three. It's nice to have two people around. When you have more than two people working together it gets a bit unfocused as an idea. We tend to pair off a little bit. It was nice on this album because the room was laid out to write the songs. We'd work with a topline writer and just write about whatever we were thinking about that day."

He also spoke about the recording process, adding: "It was crazy—we only had a month or so to record the whole album, but we always felt like we had the fans on our side. They're always anxious to know where we are—even before I do! Like today, we've been staying at the Trump Hotel all week and they've been greeting us when we leave and when we come back. It's good to see that level of dedication."

Zayn has always said he would love the opportunity to record a track with Justin Timberlake in the future. A huge Timberlake fan, he really loves his song "SexyBack." He would also like to work with Chris Brown and Katy Perry one day.The first single Zayn and the boys released from the album was "Live While We're Young." It was available on pre-order from Friday, August 24, 2012. The track was by the three songwriters who penned "What Makes You Beautiful"—Savan Kotecha, Rami Yacoub and Carl Falk.

"Live While We're Young" became the fastest-selling pre-order single ever, topping iTunes download charts in forty countries worldwide from the UK to Singapore, New Zealand to Mexico. The music video was directed by Vaughan

Arnell, the director behind videos for Robbie Williams's "Rock DJ" and the Spice Girls' "Say You'll Be There." It was filmed in the Kent countryside over two days. In the video the boys camp with their friends and have lots of fun playing soccer, riding in a jeep, having water fights, playing with inflatable balls and going for a dip in a paddling pool. Although great fun, it wasn't at all glamorous—it got pretty cold while they messed around in the water.

After filming finished, Niall tweeted, "Guys! We have literally just finished shooting the video for "live while we're young' ur gona love it! It was soo fun to shoot!"

Harry tweeted, "Day two finished, and that's the video for "Live While We're Young" done. Amazing crew, amazing people involved. Thanks again."

Originally, the boys had been planning for the video to be released on September 24, but ended up releasing it four days earlier after someone posted a rough version online. In a statement, they said: "We wanted our fans to see the video and hear the single in the proper way so we've moved the premiere to tonight. We're really excited about LWWY, we've worked really hard on it and we can't wait for everyone to see and hear it later today!"

Ultimately, the video for "Live While We're Young" was watched 8.24 million times in the first twenty-four hours of its release—a Vevo record!

Take Me Home – Track by Track

Track 1 – "Live While We're Young" – Written by Rami Yacoub, Carl Falk and Savan Kotecha. Produced by Rami Yacoub and Carl Falk.

Track 2 – "Kiss You" – Written by Rami Yacoub, Carl Falk, Savan Kotecha, Shellback, Kristian Lundin, Albin Nedler and Kristoffer Fogelmark. Produced by Rami Yacoub and Carl Falk.

Track 3 – "Little Things" – Written by Ed Sheeran and Fiona Bevan. Produced by Jake Gosling.

Track 4 – "C'mon, C'mon" – Written by Jamie Scott, John Ryan and Julian Bunetta. Produced by John Ryan and Julian Bunetta.

Track 5 – "Last First Kiss" – Written by Albin Nedler, Kristoffer Fogelmark, Rami Yacoub, Carl Falk, Savan Kotecha, Liam, Zayn and Louis. Produced by Rami Yacoub, Carl Falk, Albin Nedler and Kristoffer Fogelmark.

Track 6 – "Heart Attack" – Written by Rami Yacoub, Carl Falk, Savan Kotecha, Shellback and Kristian Lundin. Produced by Rami Yacoub, Carl Falk and Shellback.

Track 7 – "Rock Me" – Written by Lukasz Gottwald, Henry Walter, Peter Svensson, Allan Grigg and Sam Hollander. Produced by Dr. Luke, Kool Kojak and Cirkut.

Track 8 – "Change My Mind" – Written by Rami Yacoub, Carl Falk and Savan Kotecha. Produced by Rami Yacoub and Carl Falk.

Track 9 – "I Would" – Written by Tom Fletcher, Danny

Jones and Dougie Poynter. Produced by Julian Bunetta, Sam Waters and John Ryan.

Track 10 – "Over Again" – Written by Ed Sheeran, Robert Conlon and Alexander Gowers. Produced by Jake Gosling.

Track 11 – "Back for You" – Written by Kristoffer Fogelmark, Savan Kotecha, Albin Nedler, Rami Yacoub, Carl Falk, Liam, Harry, Louis and Niall. Produced by Rami Yacoub, Carl Falk, Albin Nedler and Kristoffer Fogelmark.

Track 12 – "They Don't Know About Us" – Written by Tebey Ottoh, Tommy Lee James, Peter Wallevik and Tommy P. Gregersen. Produced by Tebey Ottoh, Julian Bunetta and John Ryan.

Track 13 – "Summer Love" – Written by Steve Robson, Wayne Hector, Lindy Robbins and 1D. Produced by Steve Robson.

Bonus tracks:

Track 14 – "She's Not Afraid" – Written by Jamie Scott, John Ryan and Julian Bunetta. Produced by John Ryan and Julian Bunetta.

Track 15 – "Loved You First" – Written by Tebey Ottoh, Julian Bunetta, John Ryan and Tommy Lee James. Produced by John Ryan and Julian Bunetta.

Track 16 – "Nobody Compares" – Wwritten by Rami Yacoub, Carl Falk, Savan Kotecha and Shellback. Produced by Rami Yacoub, Carl Falk and Shellback.

Track 17 – "Still the One" – Written by Rami Yacoub, Carl Falk, Savan Kotecha, Liam, Louis and Harry. Produced by Rami Yacoub, Carl Falk and Shellback

WHAT THE REVIEWERS THOUGHT:

James Robertson from the *Mirror* wrote: " . . . with tracks written by the genius Ed Sheeran and McFly's Tom Fletcher, this was never going to be a predictable pop album. There are some obvious rhymes and repetitive tones but the five-piece have smashed it with *Take Me Home*.

"It's fun, infectious and they've found the balance between poptastic fun for the pre-teens and lyrics with meaning for embarrassed twenty-somethings who secretly listen to *Up All Night* on their iPods."

The *HitFix.com* reviewer loved the album, writing: "The tunes, tailor-made for the 2013 arena tour the quintet has already sold out, are slightly more sophisticated than the tracks on *Up All Night*, but to the band's credit, they in no way attempt to leave behind the audience that made them so popular.

"There's a song factory working overtime that churns this stuff out and the overlords have names like Dr. Luke, Shellback and Ed Sheeran: in other words, 1D has the top pop crafters in the land coming up with these tunes."

Billboard.com's reviewer wrote: "Following the massive success of *Up All Night* and the single "What Makes You Beautiful," the *X Factor* judge and band advisor challenged pop's most dominant songwriters and producers to bring their A-game to One Direction's follow-up. A glance at the album's liner notes shows some familiar faces and some new ones, but most importantly, at least half of *Take Me Home*'s songs sound like potential singles, ranging from glossy electro-pop to sentimental acoustic ballads. Even with so many producers lending a hand, there isn't a dud to be found on the record's thirteen tracks. At worst, some of the lesser cuts sound like photocopies of their stronger counterparts, which is certainly a forgivable offence for the boys of One Direction."

WHAT THE FANS THOUGHT:

Ten-year-old Charlotte thought it was not just the songs the boys released as singles that were good. She really loved "Summer Love" and would give it 5 out of 5 stars, saying: "For me, 'Summer Love' has to be one of the best songs on the album and I'm gutted it wasn't released as a single as I would have loved to have seen a music video for this song. The boys really showed how talented they are as songwriters with 'Summer Love' as the lyrics are just perfect."

This track was actually Zayn's favorite from the album and he told MTV, back in November 2012: "I really like 'Summer Love' because it's kind of different from anything we've done before. It's a cool ballad and a really great concept. I think everyone has kind of been through that experience and can relate to that song."

Superfan Sarah said: "I like "Summer Love" but I love 'Last First Kiss' more because it's a love song written by Zayn, Liam and Louis and 'Loved You First' from the *Yearbook* edition of the album because it makes me want to dance along with my friends. This album is so good, I wasn't sure if I would like it as much as *Up All Night* before I bought it, but the boys really did well to produce tracks just as catchy as those on their first album. It was nice to see that they had had more of an input on the songs themselves and I absolutely adore the cover art for the album—it's become so iconic."

Zayn let Perrie and her Little Mix bandmates, Jade, Jesy and Leigh-Anne, hear a sneak preview of the album before it was released. Jade confessed to Capital FM in July 2012: "I heard one. We heard a cheeky little song, but we're not allowed to say anything. It's brilliant—the fans will love it!"

Leigh-Anne added that she would like One Direction and Little Mix to do a track together one day: "I think it would be really interesting—a Little Mix and One Direction [song]. Imagine what that would be like."

Sadly, the girls never got their wish before Zayn left the group in March 2015, although an unofficial mash up of the boys' "Rock Me" and the girls' "DNA" was created by mash up master Earlvin14 in June 2013. It's well worth checking out on YouTube.

The boys went to Farley Hill in Henley-on-Thames to take promotional shots for the album and this is where they did their iconic phonebooth cover shot. Part of the reason why they chose the title, *Take Me Home*, is because of how much they missed home when they were traveling. For the album cover they had Liam lying on top of a red phonbooth, with his legs dangling down, while Louis sits on Zayn's shoulder, reaching up to grab Liam's arm so he doesn't fall off. Niall is inside, making a call, and Harry stands outside, with his arms crossed. Fans loved it the second they saw it.

Zayn revealed to a Vevo backstage camera: "Today is Wednesday, July 11, (2012). We're doing a photo shoot today for our next album. Six a.m. start, got up, drove here; we've just been getting changed, getting into our looks . . . Found a golf buggy, decided to take that out for a bit."

Take Me Home was released on November 9, 2012 in Australia, Germany and the Netherlands. The other release dates were: November 12 (UK), November 13 (US) and November 14 (Japan). It was Number 1 in the US, Australia, Belgium, Canada, Croatia, the Czech Republic, Denmark, Greece, Ireland, Italy, Mexico, the Netherlands, New Zealand, Norway, Portugal, Sweden, Switzerland, Taiwan, the UK and many more countries (thirty-one in total). In Austria, Brazil, Finland, Germany and Hungary it was Number 2 and Number 3 in France, Japan, Poland and Spain.

When Zayn and the other boys performed "Little Things," "What Makes You Beautiful" and "Live While We're Young" on *The Today Show* in November 2012, it was crazy. The show's presenter Matt Lauer told them: "We have never, ever had a crowd this big. This one breaks all the records." More than 15,000 fans had turned up, just to catch a glimpse of the boys performing their new material. Niall told them: "We are going to do our first ever movie and it's going to be in 3D and it's coming to cinemas near you on August 30, 2013." At this the fans screamed even louder!

The album set two records in America as 1D were the first British group to have both their first and second albums debut at Number 1 in the charts and it was an American iTunes pre-order record as fans pre-ordered an incredible 130,000 albums. *Take Me Home* was also Number 1 in the UK album chart and "Little Things" went to Number 1 in the UK singles chart at the same time. It was an amazing achievement and as soon as Zayn's mom Trisha found out, she texted him a message, saying: "Congratulations, superstar" and he replied "Thanks, mom and pop."

She also texted: "We're so happy, and that's not a little thing—no pun intended."

The whole family had been listening to *The Official Chart Show* on Radio 1 and when they found out, they danced around the kitchen in excitement. They were all so proud of Zayn and kept the newspaper and magazine cuttings for him so that he could read about himself and the boys on his next visit home. The second single from *Take Me Home* that the boys released was "Little Things," written by Fiona Bevan and Ed Sheeran. The video was directed by Vaughan Arnell, who shot the boys simply in black-and-white, singing the song in a Surrey recording studio on October 15, 2012. In the video, Niall, Liam and Louis play guitar. Arnell explained to MTV: "When I first heard the track, the mix on it was so simple and so pure and you could hear all the qualities of the voices on the track. I just wanted to come up with something that when the viewer watched it, it was almost like sitting there listening to the boys sing the track."

Altogether the video took twelve hours to film, with the boys having to sing over and over so Arnell could get shots from every angle. It must have been very tiring and difficult to stay focused for that length of time. Zayn didn't mind, though, and tweeted the next day: "Shooting video for little things was fun yesterday! Nice and sunny today, how is every1 doing? :) x."

Fans got to see the video for the first time on November 2 and "#LittleThingsOnVEVO" soon became the Number 1 trending topic on Twitter worldwide. Released on November 12, 2012, it was Number 1 in the UK, Number 2 in Ireland and New Zealand, Number 5 in Israel, Number 9 in Australia and charted well in other countries, too.

The third single they released was "Kiss You," the second single from the album to be released in Germany and the US. "Kiss You" was written by a team of songwriters that included Savan Kotecha, Carl Falk and Rami Yacoub. Shot at the same studio where *Star Wars* was filmed, in Borehamwood, Hertfordshire, the video couldn't have been more different to the *Little Things* video. High-energy and fun, it showed the boys goofing around and was once again directed by Vaughan Arnell. This time he had them recreate scenes from famous music videos using a green screen. They did their own take on Elvis Presley's "Jailhouse Rock" and the Beach Boys' "Surfer Girl."

Liam told MTV why they had decided that the track should be their second release in the US. He explained: "With the album, that's the first one that we listened to and we were like, 'Yeah, we love this song.'

"It holds a special place in our heart, I think, for this album, and it kind of sets the tone, I think, for the album."

Zayn added: "I think the whole concept behind the video is bigger than anything we've done before. It's a whole idea and it's kind of structured, which is a little bit different than what we've done before in, like, a comedy way. It's really funny—we are just having fun."

The song peaked at Number 7 in Ireland, Number 9 in the UK, Number 13 in Australia, Mexico and New Zealand, and Number 46 in the US.

At the end of 2012, when Zayn was interviewed by Billboard.com he struggled to answer a question about what his highlights of the year had been: "It is so hard to put into words what 2012 has meant to us. Last year was an amazing year for us, but when our debut album went to Number 1 [in the US], we were blown away by that. We didn't expect any of the support to the kind of level we were getting out there in the UK. And then we come out eight months later with our second album over here and it goes to Number 1 again. Things like that don't happen and we know that. We're incredibly humbled by that. Wow, what can we say except for thank you to the fans who went out and bought it."

He had also loved having the opportunity to act in the hit Nickelodeon show *iCarly*, starring Miranda Cosgrove. When the boys turned up at the TV studios, they were greeted by some five hundred fans, who had found out they were filming an episode and wanted the opportunity to meet them. Zayn has always loved acting and although he was playing himself on the show, he still had to use the acting skills he'd picked up at school. The episode aired on TV for the first time on April 7, 2012 and was seen by an audience of 3.9 million.

That same month, the boys also appeared on *Saturday Night Live*, as the episode's musical guests. This appearance was even more daunting because over 37 million people tune in each week; even some big actors and actresses have failed to make the right impression on the show because they failed to make the audience laugh. The host that night was actress Sofia Vergara, who plays Gloria in *Modern Family*. The boys performed "One Thing" and "What Makes You Beautiful" and took part in a sketch where they had to wear wigs and moustaches. Check it out on YouTube if you haven't seen it already—it's really funny!

After the show, Niall tweeted, "SNL tonight was amazing. Thanks to @nbcsnl for having us. Much appreciated!"

Harry added, "Thank you so much to @nbcsnl for having us. That was a lot of fun and we'll never forget it."

One moment that Zayn will never forget is when 1D performed at the 2012 Royal Variety Performance on November 19, and how it felt to shake the Queen's hand afterwards. They performed "Little Things" on specially created light boxes, with Zayn in the middle. To start the song, knowing that millions of people were watching the historic show, was a big moment for Zayn and the other boys. Only the very best acts are invited to perform at a Royal Variety show and it was the hundred-year anniversary so it was such a special night. Other performers who shared the stage included the legendary Rod Stewart, Neil Diamond, Robbie Williams, Girls Aloud, Kylie Minogue, Alicia Keys and Andrea Bocelli. Having to line up afterward and wait for Her Majesty the Queen to make her way down the line, chatting to the performers, must have been nerve-wracking, but Zayn did so well. It's not every day you get to meet the Queen of England and shake her hand!

Performing at the London 2012 Olympic Games Closing Ceremony on August 12, one billion people watching, was certainly a once-in-a-lifetime experience. Zayn and the other 1D boys sang "What Makes You Beautiful" on top of a truck as it circled the inside of the stadium. His family were so proud of him and Perrie gushed to the British morning television show *Daybreak,* "I think it was amazing—the boys did so well. I think everyone was amazing. I was just sitting in the audience thinking I'm so proud to be British and just to be there—the ceremony was incredible . . . I loved it."

Niall tweeted after the ceremony, "That was unbelievable, highlight of our career, and the biggest audience we will ever play to one billion people! #ThankYouLondon2012."

But Zayn didn't just enjoy performing at the Olympics, he was a spectator, too, and had tweeted throughout the Games. After seeing the opening ceremony, he had tweeted: "Thought the olympic opening ceremony yesterday was amazing, what do you guys think? X," and the next day, "Afternoon every1, watching Olympic canoeing, pretty cool :) x."

He had made good use of his all-access pass and had been to the top of the Orbit tower, watched a water polo match and snuck into the Aquatics Center even though it was closed to the public at the time.

The boys attended several award shows in 2012 but one of their greatest victories was at the MTV Video Music Awards in LA on September 6, 2012, where they picked up three awards: Best New Artist, Best Pop Video and Most Share-Worthy Video (all for "What Makes You Beautiful"). They performed "One Thing" and admit now that attending the VMAs made them think they had arrived—they never expected to win the awards and right up until the last minute had been asking fans to vote. The person they enjoyed meeting most was Lil Wayne, although Niall would say Katy Perry because they kissed on the lips! Simon Cowell was very proud, tweeting the bandmates to say, "Congratulations 1D. I'm very proud of you. Celebrate!"

Celebrate they certainly did, as after they'd won their first award Zayn and Niall had a chat in their dressing room. Zayn told Niall: "There's no way we can win a MTV Video Music Award and go home." Niall agreed and so the two of them attended Justin Bieber's after-show party and stayed in the US for a few more days before catching a flight back to the UK. Zayn hurt his foot during their extended stay and when the paparazzi took lots of photos at the airport, he decided to reassure Directioners that he was okay. He tweeted: "Hey guys, just to let you all know I'm all good, no need to worry aha.

"Just wanna take a moment to thank you guys for being so amazing.

"I've said it so many times but ill say it again, you really are the best fans in the world, thank you for being so incredible. Love you all :x."

CHAPTER TWELVE

MIDNIGHT MEMORIES

2012 might have been a great year for Zayn and the rest of the 1D boys but 2013 would be even better. On February 20, together with Harry, Liam, Louis and Niall, Zayn attended the BRIT Awards, where they were presented with the Global Success award. The person tasked with introducing the award and handing it over was none other than Robbie Williams, with whom they had performed on the *X Factor* final. Previously, they had won the Best Single award in 2012 for "What Makes You Beautiful" but this was a much bigger award. On the red carpet Capital FM asked Zayn if he was nervous. He replied: "Yeah, massively . . . We're up against some massive names, we're just honored to be here."

On the night they also performed their mash up of the Blondie song "One Way Or Another," and The Undertones' "Teenage Kicks"—their Comic Relief charity single, which was released on February 17, 2013. A cover of Blondie and The Undertones, it went to Number 1 in sixty-three countries.

Zayn was thrilled with the success because it raised thousands of pounds for a worthy cause. The boys actually visited Ghana in January 2013 to see how the money would be spent and Zayn broke down in tears when he witnessed the suffering and poverty of children in the slums. While in Ghana, the boys filmed a short video so that clips of their trip could be shown on the Comic Relief TV program. In one, Zayn pleads with the viewers watching to do something, saying: "It's so hard. I've never seen anything, never experienced anything like this in my life. The babies aren't even a year old.

"We all waste money but the most important thing we can all do is give £5 to protect children from these illnesses."

Zayn only spent two days in Ghana but what he saw will be something he will never forget and he continues to raise money for good causes. Afterward he told *Daybreak*: "It kind of put things into perspective for me, just in, like in everyday life you have, like, little problems that we think are so major, and then you go over there and you actually see people that are actually dealing with real problems."

Perrie was immensely proud of Zayn: to raise so much money for Comic Relief was a huge achievement and she knew how much his visit to Ghana had touched him. She really wished the press would print more of these positive stories and stop giving him such a hard time, particularly when it came to references to the cheating claims made by an Australian waitress in January.

The Sun had printed an interview with the Australian waitress in January 2013, claiming Zayn had cheated on Perrie with her. Alongside her story, the waitress had provided photos of Zayn shirtless and lying in bed, but fans wanted to believe she had made the whole thing up. The girl had been invited back to Zayn's place by his friend Leon Anderson and some more people Leon had met in a club. She said in the interview that at first she didn't know who Zayn was and didn't know he was in a relationship with Perrie. When the news broke neither Zayn nor Perrie released a statement, preferring not to dignify it with a response.

Although she didn't speak directly about the allegations, Perrie did tell a journalist from the *Mirror* just a few weeks later: "I try not to let what I read in the paper get to me but I still read things and I think, 'That didn't happen.' But as long as me and the rest of the girls [her bandmates] know it's not true, that's what matters. We laugh about things and refuse to let it get to us.

"Zayn is my best friend and I've seen more of him since we finished our tour, but it's hard as One Direction have been on tour as well."

She had received a few negative tweets from a small group of Directioners but was trying her best to ignore them, adding:

"It is hard when fans say nasty things on Twitter but we are starting to build a thicker skin and are getting used to it. It comes with the territory and you have to deal with it. A lot of 1D fans are our fans as well and most are very supportive of us."

At the time the media seemed obsessed with suggesting that Zayn was struggling to cope with fame and claimed bosses were concerned. Various "sources" claimed he was struggling with the pressure and had been avoiding nights out with the rest of the boys. They added that he was sick of everything he did being scrutinized and that the workload was too great. Zayn never responded to the reports and instead concentrated on putting on a united front with Perrie. No matter what the reports might have said, he was still enjoying being part of One Direction.

Music legend Elton John didn't like the way the press was treating the boys at this time and so he defended them in an interview with the *Mail on Sunday*'s *Event* magazine: "If you ignore the young or the old you are doomed. They are a great British pop band. I just hope they are getting good money because they are working bloody hard.

"I like their songs. I think they are at the age where it doesn't matter if you don't sleep because you are just enjoying the fame so much."

Sir Elton strongly believes that people with talent shouldn't get lost in the "celebrity world" and need to remember how they got there. This resonates with Zayn and the rest of the boys, who never wanted to be celebrities and have always wanted to be known for their music instead.

In 2013 the boys embarked on their worldwide Take Me Home Tour, which began in England in February 2013 and ended in Tokyo in November 2013. The tour included concerts in the UK, Ireland, France, Belgium, the Netherlands, Germany, Denmark, Norway, Sweden, Switzerland, Italy, Spain, Portugal, Mexico, America, Canada, Australia and New Zealand.

Set list

"Up All Night"
"I Would"
"Heart Attack"
"More Than This"
"Loved You First"
"One Thing"
"C'mon, C'mon"
"Change My Mind"
"One Way Or Another (Teenage Kicks)"
"Last First Kiss"
"Moments"
"Back For You"
"Summer Love"
"Over Again"
"Little Things"
"Teenage Dirtbag" (Wheatus cover)
"Rock Me"
"She's Not Afraid"
"Kiss You"
"Live While We're Young"
"Best Song Ever"
"What Makes You Beautiful"

For their gigs in the UK, North America, Australia and New Zealand, the boys were supported by the band 5 Seconds of Summer; in Europe they were supported by singer Camryn and their friend Olly Murs joined them in Japan.

The Take Me Home Tour was much bigger than the Up All Night Tour; they put on 123 shows over eight months. When the boys went to Japan in January 2013 to announce that they would be finishing the tour there, they had a great time and on arrival, did a bit of late-night karaoke. They sang songs by Backstreet Boys, Jay Z, Kenny Rogers and 50 Cent. The next day at the press conference they were all feeling a bit exhausted after a late night and needed to adjust to the time difference (the flight had been eleven hours long). Zayn was feeling terrible and after twenty minutes had to leave so he could be sick.

Their schedule in Japan was crammed with performances and interviews but they did have a small amount of free time. Zayn bought himself a hi-tech robot and sampled some tofu and sashimi. All the boys enjoyed visiting a noodle bar but they struggled to understand what was on the menu because of course it was all in Japanese. They enjoyed wearing matching red kimonos during their visit, too.

Zayn did enjoy traveling around the world as part of 1D but sometimes it became a bit too much and he just wanted a break. After a long stretch on the road, he often tired of living out of a suitcase and staying in hotel rooms, even if they were totally luxurious. He found long interview days tiring and wished that he could explore some of the amazing places they visited rather than just see the inside of hotel rooms and TV studios. However, he always tried to make the most of any days off in a new country, by visiting landmarks and tourist spots.

Even on days when he was feeling homesick and under the weather he never let this impact on his performance. After all, fans attending a 1D concert wanted to see the boys messing around and having a laugh, as well as performing great songs. Zayn made sure that they never left disappointed. In April 2013, Brian Friedman, the choreographer who had worked with the boys on *The X Factor*, told *Heat* magazine that Zayn still wasn't a natural dancer: "He's got rhythm, he can't learn choreography. He gets really intimidated and scared and can't remember it."

When asked whether he thought One Direction should do more dance routines, Friedman replied: "Absolutely not! They didn't do too well with dancing when I was working with them.

"It's not that they can't handle it—some are better than others, no names to be mentioned—but it's not what they're about. They're not a dancey boy band kind of thing, they're just about youth and exuberance and making girls swoon."

In fact, 1D never wanted to be a boy band that danced a lot, they just wanted to concentrate on singing. Zayn revealed to *Glamour* magazine in July 2013: "We didn't want to just follow the boy band formula. We didn't want to do any dancing, we just wanted to be five dudes in a band." Liam added: "We can't dance—we're a bit lazy. We're just normal lads, we look stupid dancing. That's what I think."

During one of their performances in Chicago, Zayn had to come to the rescue when Harry almost walked into a pyrotechnic torch. He was walking towards the flames while wiping sweat from his face with a towel and couldn't see. Zayn quickly dashed over and pulled him away from it—a couple of steps further and Harry might have set his hair alight. If you want to see what happened for yourself, you can check it out on YouTube.

By the time the bandmates were performing their last show in Australia on October 30, 2013 they were feeling very emotional, having been in the country for a month. Zayn, Harry and Niall all seemed overcome with emotion at different points during the performance, which showed just how much of an emotional roller coaster they'd been on. By then Zayn was desperate to see Perrie and his family face to face.

When interviewed for *The X Factor Australia* the boys had been asked what they would do if that day was their last day on earth. Zayn said he would go and see his family, Harry thought he would go for a hot-air balloon ride and Louis said they would all skydive into their families' houses.

Once the tour was over, the boys couldn't just chill out indefinitely as they had to prepare for 1D Day on November 23—a seven-hour livestream event for fans hosted by the band, which would see them interview special guests, take part in amusing challenges, perform new tracks, try to break world records and lots more.

The boys filmed the show in Los Angeles and they had their own special set with seating areas, an interactive area to talk to people online and a band area with their musicians, Josh Devine, Dan Richards, Jon Shone and Sandy Beales. For the first and the last hour of 1D Day they hosted together, but for the rest of the time they were paired up.

For the second hour it was Liam and Harry's turn to be in charge, Niall and Louis took charge of the third hour, while Zayn and Liam had the fourth hour and for the fifth hour it was Harry and Niall, then Zayn and Louis for the sixth hour. The idea of pairing them off was so that the members of the group who weren't on for a particular slot could have a rest but that didn't happen because they wanted to watch what was going on. They had all been given scripts so they would know what was going to happen and when, but they hadn't really had enough time to prepare properly.

The boys were under an immense amount of pressure as they had 32 million fans watching the show worldwide, but they took it all in their stride. Highlights included a clip of them working out topless on tour, seeing Zayn's graffiti skills, Piers Morgan asking them difficult questions, Niall dyeing his hair lilac, Harry squeezing into a phone box with two fans, and the whole group singing "White Christmas" with Canadian singer-songwriter Michael Bublé . . . There were so many good bits! A couple of moments didn't work— the live hook-ups with *X Factor* and *Doctor Who* didn't quite go to plan and the show overran, being eight hours long instead of seven (not that anyone minded!). As soon as it was over many fans wanted to know when the next one was, and they looked forward to seeing the "Best Bits" videos on YouTube.

Aside from touring, one of Zayn's highlights of 2013 was unveiling his own waxwork model in Madame Tussauds London. It had been a complete surprise when he learned that he and the other boys had been chosen to be made into waxworks, as they were visiting Madame Tussauds at the time. He never expected it because you have to be a legend to be included. Each individual model costs £150,000 (over $200,00) to make as they must be exact replicas. Even though 1D were huge stars by this point, Zayn still thought of them as being normal lads. They had meetings with the waxwork creators and casts were taken to ensure the finished waxworks were as lifelike as possible.

During their trip the boys picked out their favorite waxworks. Zayn chose Bob Marley, Louis couldn't decide between the members of The Beatles, Harry picked Gandhi, Niall went for Rihanna and Liam opted for the Arnold Schwarzenegger waxwork.

Before the 1D models were unveiled, principal sculptor Stephen Mansfield revealed in a video for the Madame Tussauds' website: "We are acutely aware that millions of fans around the world will have a lot to say about these figures and we are determined not to let them down. We are hard at work to not only recreate totally accurate physical likenesses, but we want to inject something of the boys' energy and personalities into their figures too. The boys have been a delight to work with, really co-operative and a huge amount of fun."

The waxworks were available for viewing in Madame Tussauds London from April 28 to July 11, 2013, before being transported to Madame Tussauds New York in the heart of Times Square, for American fans to check them out from July 19 to October 11, 2013. They then went all the way to Madame Tussauds Sydney, Australia, from October 2,4 2013 to January 28, 2014.

Waxworks of Zayn, Niall, Liam, Louis and Harry all had their arms covered with long sleeves to prevent the models from becoming dated since the boys are constantly adding tattoos to their arms. Their clothing was updated in August 2014 and after Zayn left the band Madame Tussauds announced they had no plans to remove him from the lineup. Meanwhile, One Direction fans were eager to have another album to listen to and for obvious reasons the boys' record company didn't want to disappoint, so the bandmates had to fit in writing and recording their third album, *Midnight Memories*, while busying themselves on the Take Me Home Tour.

But before they offered the album for sale, they decided to release two tracks in advance. "Best Song Ever" was released on July 22, 2013 and "Story Of My Life" came out on October 28, 2013.

During their trip to Miami in June 2013, the boys had three days of shows, they had to film the video for "Best Song Ever" and then there was one day off. While there, they stayed at The Ritz-Carlton Key Biscayne. Niall and Harry tried to sunbathe by the pool before they had to be at the American Airlines Arena each night for the show. There were lots of fans in the hotel, watching their every move, which deterred Zayn from joining them. He confessed to Dana Mathews from *Teen Vogue* in July 2013 that he still couldn't swim, saying: "It was a bit too busy for me [by the pool]. I like to chill somewhere quiet. I get pleasure from the little things in life."

There was a good deal of hype before "Best Song Ever" was released, with lots of people wrongly presuming Zayn and the other boys were being arrogant by saying it was the best song ever recorded, when the title actually refers to the line in the song's chorus: "And we danced all night to the best song ever . . . " (Incidentally, the start of "Best Song Ever" features a sample of "Baba O'Riley" by The Who.)

Harry loved the track and told Radio 1's Scott Mills: "'Best Song Ever' is my favorite song that we have done so far . . . it's kind of a little bit heavier. We're not like Slipknot or anything, but bigger and bigger—the drums are bigger, the guitars are bigger. And I really like it."

The video was a huge hit and broke the Vevo record for most views within twenty-four hours on YouTube with 12.3 million views, but was ultimately beaten by Miley Cyrus's infamous *Wrecking Ball* video in September 2013, which got 19.3 million views.

Just half an hour after the *Best Song Ever* video, the trailer for the boys' movie, *This Is Us*, was released so fans had two great things they could watch repeatedly. Though, the trailer included a snippet from *Best Song Ever* video, for many it couldn't beat the watchability of the actual music video, which had Zayn cross-dressing as secretary Veronica!

The video had been written by comedian James Corden and the director Ben Winston. Corden is a good friend of One Direction and had invited them all to be guests at his wedding the year before. He was the perfect person to come up with a unique concept that would require the boys to act and be extremely funny at the same time.

Perrie was a huge fan of Veronica, tweeting: "The #BestSongEver video is my absolute fave!

"Slightly worried that my new girl crush might be my boyfriend! #Iwould ;) aha, LOVEIT Perrie <3."

Zayn's fans were happy to read Perrie's tweets because it confirmed that they were still very much in love. Only recently, Zayn had flown in and out of the UK in just two days to see her.

But Zayn wasn't the only member of the group to have to dress up for "Best Song Ever"—every one of them had a different part. Louis and Niall played studio executives Jonny and Harvey, and Harry was marketing guy Marcel, while Liam played Leeroy the choreographer. The transformations were amazing, with wigs, padded suits and bald caps helping Louis and Niall to become fifty-something overweight men. Zayn's transformation was undoubtedly the biggest, and the way Louis and Liam check out his backside when his back is turned is hilarious, as is Harry's flirting. This was a truly feel-good video, with fans loving the energy One Direction and their characters have as they sing "Best Song Ever" while causing chaos in the office!

The video was filmed in an art-deco style mansion in Miami Beach, Florida, called Temple House. A highly desirable location for celebrities, it has been hired by Jennifer Lopez, Jay Z, Jamie Foxx and the Kardashians, to name just a few. Temple House owner Daniel Davidson issued a press release after the boys filmed the video, saying: "I grew up riveted to The Beatles—One Direction is on a trajectory that takes their beats and messages to the world in every channel, including voracious fans behind additional social media stardom. Watching the One Direction band members behind the scenes, they are one hundred percent authentic, playful, fun, and wildly talented. It was incredible to watch the entire team. [director] Ben, [executive producer] Luti and [director of photography] Maz work seamlessly together to orchestrate and capture the remarkable energy and magic of One Direction."

Producer Luti Fagbenle added: "The Temple House was the perfect private hideaway for the boys. They hung out shirtless at Dan's private second-floor pool deck between takes, safely tucked away from the throngs of adoring fans."

Fans could pre-order "Best Song Ever" from June 26, and it was released on July 22, 2013. When it made Number 2 in the US charts, the 1D boys were more than pleased because they knew they wouldn't be able to knock Robin Thicke and "Blurred Lines" off the top spot. The bandmates shared with *Access Hollywood* how surprised they'd been on the day of the shoot to walk into the room and see Zayn as a girl—they hadn't know what to expect and it had freaked them out quite a bit! Filming the video had been strange because they didn't film the scenes in sequence and had had to film some scenes numerous times as their characters had to pose questions in character and then answer as themselves. Zayn revealed that when they found out they were Number 2, Niall had "done a little jump and his knee dislocated and relocated."

Liam added: "That's our highest debut so we were so happy with it. It's always a bit strange when you come out with new stuff because you don't know, and especially when you've changed the sound 'round a little bit, but we were really happy with the record."

The song did well in other countries, too. It was Number 2 in the UK, Canada, Denmark, Ireland, Turkey and Venezuela, Number 3 in Italy and New Zealand and Number 4 in Australia, Hungary and Mexico.

Their next single was "Story Of My Life," which was released on October 28, 2013. Fans heard it first on the radio on November 25, and saw the video for the single on November 3, 2013. On the day of its radio debut Niall told Capital FM: "This track is not actually one that we wrote this time. A good friend of ours and a songwriter called Jamie Scott, who's in a band called Graffti6, he wrote this song. He's written a few for us before, like 'More Than This,' and on the last few albums.

"He's written a lot with us on this album, too. We were in Nottingham on tour when we were touring the UK, back in February and March, and we just came into a room one day and he was like, 'I've got this song that I've written and I want to play you.' And we just fell in love with it the second we heard it."

The bandmates put their unique stamp on the song, with Scott confessing to MTV a few days later: "The boys have really good voices, they've all got very different voices. Harry [Styles's] rasp is something that you can always lean towards . . . All the boys have such a great sound themselves . . . for instance, the demo that we played the boys sounds a lot more folky than it does now. That's what amazing about their voices [when they record a song]—straightaway, it sounds like them.

"I think I probably enjoyed writing this song the most of any track we've written for the boys, and with the boys. It had a real timeless thing to it and I think it's something you can hear being played in ten years' time."

The video quickly became a firm favorite with fans; they loved seeing the boys recreate photos from their childhoods with their families. It was their most personal to date, with fans particularly enjoying Zayn's scenes with his sister Waliyha. In the video the boys develop photos from their family albums in a darkroom and the photos are then updated to the present day. The saddest scene is of Louis with his grandparents. When the photo is updated, two of his grandparents are no longer present as they have passed away.

Many people expected the song to hit Number 1 in the UK, as it was leading the chart all week in the run-up, but it ended peaking at Number two, losing out to Eminem and Rihanna's "The Monster." It did, however, reach the top spot in other countries: Number 1 in Bulgaria, Denmark, Ireland, the Lebanon, Mexico and Spain. It was also Number 3 in Australia, Belgium, Canada, Greece, Israel, the Netherlands, Scotland and Turkey. In the US, it reached Number 6.

When it came to announcing what the album was to be called, the boys decided to have fun, using social media to build excitement. On September 6, Niall tweeted: "Guys! We have an exciting album announcement for ya at 4PM today." A couple of hours later, Zayn tweeted "What is @ harry_styles up to? :)" with a link to a YouTube video. When fans clicked onto the link they saw Harry rearranging pieces of paper on a floor, with a letter written on each one. When arranged in the right order, the pieces of paper would spell out "Midnight Memories." After giving the fans time to try and solve the puzzle, the boys tweeted from their @one-direction account: "YES – 1D's 3rd album is MIDNIGHT MEMORIES & is out Nov 25! AND you can pre-order Mon! 1DHQ x #RememberRememberThe25thNovember." They also added a longer Instagram video of Harry arranging the letters in the right order.

Fans were surprised by the title because they had expected the album to be called *Where We Are*—previous tours had shared their names with the corresponding albums.

As well as getting fans to guess the title, on October 11, the boys had fun trying to get them to guess the names of the tracks on the album by giving a series of clues and getting them to fill in the blanks. Called #MidnightMemoriesTrackQuiz, it was a huge hit on Twitter. The clue for their first track was easy: "#MidnightMemoriesTrack1: You helped break a @VEVO record by watching the video for this LOTS . . . 1DHQ." Fans instantly knew it was "Best Song Ever." The second track clue was "#MidnightMemoriesTrack2: The guys revealed news about this track yesterday.. 1DHQ x." Fans quickly responded with "Story Of My Life." When it came to the clue for the third track, British fans found it easier to guess because it referred to a former UK *X Factor* contestant: "#MidnightMemoriesTrack3: The first name of a singer whose surname is "Vickers': _ _ _ n _ 1DHQ x." The answer was Diana (for Diana Vickers, a 2008 *X Factor* semifinalist). This track was previously leaked so fans that fell in love with it as soon as they heard it had been hoping it would be featured on *Midnight Memories.*

Track 4 was ridiculously easy: "#MidnightMemoriesTrack4: Memories that happen at midnight. And this album's title. Obviously. 1DHQ x," while Track 5 proved a lesson in grammar: "#MidnightMemoriesTrack5: Not me and you. (_ _ _ & _) 1DHQ x"—answer: "You & I."

Track 6 was pretty easy to guess: "D _ _ ' t / F _ r g _ t / W _ e r _ / Y _ _ / B _ l _ n g / 1DHQ x"—answer: "Don't Forget Where You Belong." Track 7's clue was "MidnightMemoriesTrack7: The opposite of weak. 1DHQ x"—answer: "Strong." The clue for Track 8 was slightly trickier: "#MidnightMemoriesTrack8: Merrily/With enjoyment: H _ _ _ _ _ _ 1DHQ x"—answer: "Happily," while the clue for Track 9 was "#MidnightMemoriesTrack9:): Not at any other time: R _ _ _ _ / N _ _ 1DHQ x"—answer: "Right Now."

Fans really enjoyed taking part in the quiz and firing back their answers. The clue for Track 10 was "#MidnightMemoriesTrack10: Small dark colored item of girls' clothing: L _ _ _ _ _ / B _ _ _ _ / D _ _ _ _ 1DHQ x"—answer: "Little Black Dress." Track 11 was "#MidnightMemoriesTrack11: Through the _ _ _ _ (opposite of light) 1DHQ x"—answer: "Through The Dark." Track 12's clue was "#MidnightMemoriesTrack12: Something G _ _ _ _ (opposite of small/unimportant) 1DHQ x"—answer: "Something Great." Track 13's clue was one of the most difficult: "#MidnightMemoriesTrack13: Small + Pale + Non-truths 1DHQ x"—answer: "Little White Lies." Track 14's clue was tricky, too: "#MidnightMemoriesTrack14: An improvement on things that are spoken: B _t _ _ _ / T _ _ _ / W _ _ _ _"—answer: "Better Than Words."

In an interview with Capital FM in October 2013, Niall revealed what the fans should expect, saying: "People think, 'Oh, we've got a third album now, let's change it totally,' but you actually scare people off by doing that.

"We just wanted to change it up a little bit to give it more of an edge and obviously, we gained a lot more creative control. We were able to write a lot more of it.

"It's very edgy, loads of guitars, loads of drums and then obviously you've got your ballads there, too."

The *Midnight Memories* album was due to be released on November 25, 2013, but a version was leaked online a week earlier, much to the disappointment of Zayn and the rest of the boys. Liam told *Digital Spy* at the time: "It is annoying because there's this big buildup and it affects sales. We really want a number one, so we're just kind of hoping for the best now. Hopefully, people will go out and buy it."

Louis continued: "It's just frustrating when you work so hard on an album and you kind of want everyone to hear it at the same time. Some select fans won't listen to it until it's out, which is great. But there are others who obviously can't help themselves."

Despite the boys' reservations as soon as *Midnight Memories* was released, it quickly climbed to the top of the charts in almost every country. It was Number 1 in Argentina, Australia, Belgium, Canada, Croatia, Cyprus, the Czech Republic, Denmark, Greece, Hungary, Ireland, Mexico, Norway, Portugal, Spain, Sweden, Taiwan, the UK and the US. By getting to the top of the charts in the US, One Direction became the first band to have their first three albums hit Number 1 since The Monkees in 1967. In fact, first-week sales have grown with the release of every album from One Direction. *Up All Night* sold 176,000 copies, while *Take Me Home* sold 540,000 copies and *Midnight Memories* sold 546,000 copies.

With all those number ones, it's no surprise that despite only being released at the end of November, *Midnight*

Memories sold more copies worldwide than any other album of 2013. It was a tremendous boost for the band and the UK music scene in general.

Gennaro Castaldo from the British Phonographic Institute (BPI), who compile the list, told the BBC: "For home-grown talent to have recorded the world's biggest-selling album six out of the last seven years is a phenomenal achievement that says a great deal about the popularity of British music around the world.

"Aside from the obvious contribution to British exports, this success underlines the vital role that our music and artists play in promoting the appeal of British culture around the world."

BEST-SELLING ALBUMS WORLDWIDE, 2013

1. One Direction, *Midnight Memories* – 4.0 million copies sold
2. Eminem, *The Marshall Mathers LP2* – 3.8 million copies sold
3. Justin Timberlake, *The 20/20 Experience* – 3.6 million copies sold
4. Bruno Mars, *Unorthodox Jukebox* – 3.2 million copies sold
5. Daft Punk, *Random Access Memories* – 3.2 million copies sold
6. Katy Perry, *Prism* – 2.8 million copies sold
7. Michael Bublé, *To Be Loved* – 2.4 million copies sold
8. Imagine Dragons, *Night Visions* – 2.4 million copies sold
9. Lady Gaga, *Artpop* – 2.3 million copies sold
10. Beyoncé, *Beyoncé* – 2.3 million copies sold

WHAT THE REVIEWERS THOUGHT:

Midnight Memories was a more mature album than *Up All Night* and *Take Me Home* and some critics felt it was too mature for the majority of their fans. They felt it didn't have enough memorable tracks. *The Daily Telegraph* critic Neil McCormick didn't agree, awarding it four out of five stars and writing in his review: "One Direction's new album, *Midnight Memories*, is cheeky, swaggeringly confident pop rock from the boys who know they're onto a winner.

"It is all so swaggeringly confident and honed to a perfect point, it is hard not to be caught up in its own sense of conviction."

Chris Payne from Billboard.com, gave it four–and-a-half stars out of five: "For a band comprised of nineteen- to twenty-one-year-olds, growth is going to be a key theme. In general terms, *Midnight Memories* doesn't sound like much of a departure from its predecessors, but a closer look reveals hints as to what lies ahead. Guitars feature more prominently in the new songs, whether they're loud and electric ('Little Black Dress'), soft and acoustic ('Story of My Life'), or of the fast-strumming, Mumford & Sons variety ('Happily'). One Direction proves once again that there is more Jonas Brothers than *NSYNC or Backstreet Boys in their boy band DNA, and given their increased role in the writing process (the band contributed lyrics to twelve of the fourteen songs), perhaps the rock band vibe will be an even greater theme as the band grows up."

WHAT THE FANS THOUGHT:

Bobby, Gwen and Elissa are huge 1D fans. Their favorite members of the group are Harry and Louis. They love Louis for the way he sings, his football skills and the fact that he has a smiley face in his signature and Harry because he also has an amazing voice and always has a lot of time for the Directioners he meets. Here's what they say about *Midnight Memories*:

"For us, 'Best Song Ever' has to be one of the best songs on this album, it's so catchy and we can't help but smile every time we see the video. We've lost count of the amount of times we've watched it, we click the replay button so often it's a wonder we haven't broke it!"

Ten-year-old Amelia loves Liam because of his great face and the fact that he's always smiling. "I love *Midnight Memories* because of the lyrics, it's an anthem . . . If someone starts singing it near me I find it impossible not to join in. The video was absolutely brilliant—the boys were so brave, hanging over the edge of Tower Bridge. I know they were wearing harnesses, but it still took guts—especially for Zayn, who's scared of heights. It would have been easy for them to use stunt doubles but as always, they wanted to do things themselves. They are always up for pushing themselves and trying new things, and that's part of the reason why Directioners like myself love them!"

Ten-year-old Phoebe agrees: " 'Midnight Memories' melody is so catchy. Even other famous singers like Miley Cyrus have commented on how catchy it is and how it can stick in your head for weeks once you've heard it on the radio!"

Nine-year-old Olivia and ten-year-old Imogen try to look deeper, explaining, "We think when it comes down to deciding which are the best songs on the album, it comes down to which tracks have the most meaningful lyrics. For this reason 'You & I' stands out for us. We think it's one of their best ballads and when you listen to it you can't help but dream that the boys are singing directly to you.

"The setting for the video might be simple, but the way it was done was amazing and we're so glad the boys, director and those behind the scenes received recognition for it, not just from 1D fans but from the music industry as a whole."

Ten-year-old Summer agrees: "I am a huge Liam fan and I love the Big Payno remix that he did of 'You & I.' Liam is a talented songwriter and I can see him writing for big artists in the future. He is so committed to 1D and the fact that he enjoys writing songs even when he's on a day off shows how seriously he takes it."

"You & I" was actually Zayn's favorite song on the album and he told Capital FM: "It's quite slow, but it's kind of got the same sort of vibe as 'What Makes You Beautiful' in that it sticks in your head. It's really catchy. It's got that amazing melody to it where you just can't help but sing."

If you find yourself crying when you listen to "Story Of My Life" or watch the video then you're not alone. Nine-year-old Olivia adds, "It's an emotional song and takes you on a bit of an emotional roller coaster as you listen to it.

It's a great song that the boys wrote together and shows how much they have matured since their earlier two albums."

It was Niall's favorite, too: "It's up there with the best that we've brought out—'Story Of My Life' might just take it. It's a very passionate song and when you see the video that goes with it, it suits it as well."

After promoting the album around the world, the boys had a well-deserved three months off. This came as a relief to Zayn, who was desperate to spend quality time with Perrie and his family. The boys all went home to see their families and they didn't meet up again until the 2014 BRIT Awards on February 19, 2014. That night Zayn had a great time as he celebrated winning the British Video award for "Best Song Ever" and the BRITS Global Success award with his four best pals. They told journalists who suggested they might be splitting up that they were talking nonsense— while apart, they'd been WhatsApp messaging each other and discussing new songs. Liam told a reporter from *The Sun*: "I miss the boys, but if you don't see your family, you would go mad. We're writing the new album and want to make that amazing.

"We don't want to be on *The Big Reunion* [a British TV show that shows disbanded groups getting back together] next year. We don't want to be on *The Big Reunion* ever. Well, maybe in 2050."

After rehearsing for their new tour, it was time for the bandmates to release their third single from the album, "Midnight Memories." Though available to download since

November 2013, it was officially released on March 9, 2014. But it didn't do well in the UK, only managing a Number 39 position in the charts, but this was perhaps understandable given that fans had been downloading it for some time. It fared better elsewhere, reaching Number 2 in Denmark, Number 3 in Ireland and New Zealand, Number 4 in Belgium and Number 5 in Hungary and the Netherlands. The cover art was a particular hit with Zayn's fans because it had the singer in the middle, looking particularly sexy in a pair of suspenders.

Directed by Ben Winston, the accompanying video saw the boys in London at a house party and kebab shop before borrowing mobility scooters from some pensioners, stealing a police boat to ride down the River Thames and singing at the top of Tower Bridge. In the lead-up to it being shown on January 31, 2014, the bandmates released a series of videos. In the first video, which was released on January 23, Liam said: "It's actually one of the songs I wrote with Louis. This is the first song we wrote on the album so this kinda, like, paved the way for this whole album sound and the way it all changes and stuff." They built up excitement for the video by posting behind-the-scenes videos and two teaser videos showing short clips from the full video on Facebook and Twitter.

When the latter was released on the 31st, some fans of Zayn were very angry because he hadn't been given a solo in the song and he didn't appear much in the video itself. Harry sang the first verse while Louis sang the bridge with

Liam and Niall sharing the second verse. Zayn had only eleven seconds of solo screen time whereas the others had more than double that and he wasn't even prominent in the group shots. Superfan Milan tweeted: "That's not fair! y does zayn malik always gets the least solo and less time on screen in the video #MidnightMemories dats not fair."

Other fans tweeted Zayn himself to ask why he'd been snubbed: "@zaynmalik if im not mistaken, all of the boys have their own SOLO in Midnight Memories..except you. How & Why is this happening . . . ??? :("

But Zayn didn't respond to the tweets, preferring to keep thoughts on the matter to himself. Some newspapers claimed at the time that he was the least popular member of the group, which simply wasn't true. They suggested that because he played such a small role, he might even be thinking of leaving the band.

The fourth and final single from *Midnight Memories* was "You & I," which was released on May 5, 2014. On April 18, the video premiered and was once again directed by Ben Winston. This couldn't have been more different to the *Midnight Memories* video; it was very simple and gave the impression that it was all taken in one shot (although in reality it wasn't). It had the boys morph into one another as they walked along a pier until they all joined together and collected frozen stills of themselves. They filmed it on March 24 at Clevedon Pier, Somerset, much to the delight of Directioners living nearby and famously described as the "most beautiful pier in England" by poet Sir John Betjeman.

The *You & I* video went on to win the British Video award at the 2015 BRIT Awards.

In August 2014, Zayn and the boys released their third fragrance, which was called "You & I." Previously, they had released "Our Moment" in June 2013, which became the fastest-selling perfume of 2013, and "That Moment" in April 2014.

"You & I" reached Number 19 in the UK charts, Number 7 in Ireland, Number 13 in Spain and Number 17 in Belgium, however, it only mangaged to reach Number 68 in the US charts.

Despite not being officially released as singles, several of the album's promotional singles managed to do well in the download charts. "Diana" was Number 1 in Greece and Denmark, Number 2 in Australia, Ireland and New Zealand, and Number 3 in Belgium, Hungary, the Netherlands, Portugal and Spain. If you have ever wondered, "Diana" is about a certain girl but none of the boys have ever revealed her identity. Louis did admit in one interview that they had experimented with different names and for a while it was Joanna but because his mom's name is Johannah, it was just too weird!

Midnight Memories – Track by Track

Track 1 – "Best Song Ever" Written by Wayne Hector, John Ryan, Ed Drewett and Julian Bunetta. Produced by Julian Bunetta, John Ryan and Matt Rad.

Track 2 – "Story Of My Life" Written by Julian Bunetta, Jamie Scott, John Ryan and 1D. Produced by Julian Bunetta and John Ryan.

Track 3 – "Diana" Written by Julian Bunetta, Jamie Scott, John Ryan, Louis and Liam. Produced by Julian Bunetta and John Ryan.

Track 4 – "Midnight Memories" Written by Julian Bunetta, Jamie Scott, John Ryan, Louis and Liam. Produced by Julian Bunetta and John Ryan.

Track 5 – "You & I" Written by Julian Bunetta, Jamie Scott and John Ryan. Produced by Julian Bunetta and John Ryan.

Track 6 – "Don't Forget Where You Belong" Written by Tom Fletcher, Danny Jones, Dougie Poynter and Niall. Produced by Tom Fletcher, Danny Jones and Dougie Poynter.

Track 7 – "Strong" Written by Julian Bunetta, Jamie Scott, John Ryan and Louis. Produced by Julian Bunetta and John Ryan.

Track 8 – "Happily (Say 'I Love You')" Written by Savan Kotecha, Carl Falk and Harry. Produced by Carl Falk and Kristian Lundin.

Track 9 – "Right Now" Written by Ryan Tedder, Louis, Liam and Harry. Produced by Ryan Tedder and Jake Gosling.

Track 10 – "Little Black Dress" Written by Julian Bunetta, John Ryan, Theodore Geiger, Louis and Liam. Produced by Julian Bunetta, John Ryan and Theodore Geiger.

Track 11 – "Through The Dark" Written by Jamie Scott, Toby Smith, Louis and Liam. Produced by Jamie Scott, Toby Smith and John Ryan.

Track 12 – "Something Great" Written by Jacknife Lee, Gary Lightbody and Harry. Produced by Jacknife Lee.

Track 13 – "Little White Lies" Written by Wayne Hector, John Ryan, Ed Drewett, Julian Bunetta, Louis and Liam. Produced by Julian Bunetta and John Ryan.

Track 14 – "Better Than Words" Written by Julian Bunetta, Jamie Scott, John Ryan, Louis and Liam. Produced by Julian Bunetta and John Ryan.

Ultimate Edition bonus tracks:

Track 15 – "Why Don't We Go There?" Written by Steve Robson, Claude Kelly, Wayne Hector and Louis. Produced by Steve Robson.

Track 16 – "Does He Know?" Written by Julian Bunetta, Jamie Scott, John Ryan, Louis and Liam. Produced by Julian Bunetta, John Ryan and Jamie Scott.

Track 17 – "Alive" Written by Julian Bunetta, Jamie Scott, John Ryan and Louis. Produced by Julian Bunetta, John Ryan and Matt Rad.

Track 18 – "Half A Heart" was written by Steve Robson, Ed Drewett and Lindy Robbins. Produced by Steve Robson.

When one of the album's songwriters and producers, Julian Bunetta, sat down with MTV shortly before the album was released he gave an insight into some of the tracks they had created together: "['Midnight Memories'] definitely personifies their lifestyle.

"And midnight memories are where most of the memories of this record were made. [It] was between midnight and five in the morning. We have so many memories of just being in the studio or being after a show or being in the back of the bus or going to one of the guys' places and hanging and writing. Or, [it's also] just when you're young and that's when you kind of have all your experiences."

Bunetta also revealed that Liam had the inspiration for the song when he was lying on the floor in a hotel hallway with the boys, playing with his dog and beatboxing. They started working on it straightaway: "We ran into the hotel room, where the studio was set up. We laid it down and as I was making the quick little beat, Liam went [to the bathroom] and he came out and he was like, "Bro, what if we write a song using all song titles?" And I don't know who it was [but] 'Better Than Words' popped out somehow."

The 2014 Where We Are Tour started on April 25, in Bogotá, Colombia and ended on October 5, in Miami, Florida. When the tour was announced at Wembley Stadium on May 16, 2013, Harry told the press: "It's important the fans and everyone who comes to see the show know it's going to be much bigger and new songs. A completely different tour."

A journalist from MTV asked where they saw themselves in ten years' time. Liam answered: "We want to do this for as long as we can, really.

"We came to watch Take That at Wembley when they were doing their stadium tour and we couldn't believe how big it was, so if we can emulate something like that, I think that's the way to go."

Louis added: "For us, it's more about keeping our feet on the ground and taking every day as it comes. That would be great, but at the moment we are just set for the stadiums—I can't believe I'm saying it!"

This time around they performed sixty-nine shows to much greater audiences than previous tours. It did make them slightly nervous before they walked on stage each night but it gave them a massive buzz, too. Zayn once revealed that they would try to make each other laugh just before shows started to combat their nerves and would go through their own pre-show routines. He used to like to brush his teeth just before going on stage but after a while it didn't bother him whether he brushed his teeth before a show or not.

In an interview in 2012, Zayn admitted to YTV *One to One* what the boys got up to once they had done a soundcheck and had time to kill before a show was due to start. He said: "We just mess about, we're normal lads. We just mess about in our dressing rooms. We play this game called Real Fruit Ninja—basically, what you do is throw the fruit in the air and you cut it in half."

However, he warned fans not to try this at home and to get permission from an adult before touching sharp objects. The boys started playing the game because their dressing rooms always seemed to be stocked with a bowl of fruit, a knife and a chopping board.

In the same interview the other boys named Zayn as the member of 1D most likely to chill at home rather than go out partying. Niall added that on their days off, Zayn preferred staying in.[

Set list:
"Midnight Memories"
"Little Black Dress"
"Kiss You"
"Why Don't We Go There"
"Rock Me"
"Don't Forget Where You Belong"
"Live While We're Young"
"C'mon, C'mon"
"Right Now"
"Through The Dark"
"Happily"
"Little Things"
"Moments"
"Strong"
"Better Than Words"
"Alive"
"One Thing"
"Diana"
"What Makes You Beautiful"
Encore:
"You & I"
"Story Of My Life"
"Little White Lies"
"Best Song Ever"

Shortly after the tour finished, the boys' tour manager, Paul Higgins, who had been with them since the beginning and had also been like a surrogate dad to them, decided to quit. Prior to working with the band, he had worked with the likes of Westlife, Boyzone and Girls Aloud. For Paul to leave the 1D family was a huge shock—he'd always posted interesting backstage photos, tweeted about what the boys were up to and had been so nice to the fans. He never revealed why he quit.

Paul had always cared about the boys on a personal level, as well as professionally, too. He'd been right by their side from the day after the *X Factor* final. The boys went over to Ireland to see him marry his wife Clodagh in 2011 and filmed two really funny "Marryoake" videos while they were there. Zayn and the rest of the boys appear on a karaoke-style video set to "I've Gotta Feeling" by the Black Eyed Peas and Niall and Liam appear on a karaoke-style video set to Lou Reed's "Perfect Day." For Paul not to be in their lives anymore would take a while to get used to.

There had been some controversy while Zayn and the boys were on tour. In May 2014 many fans were shocked when the *Daily Mail* published a video on their website of Zayn and Louis sharing what appeared to be a joint as they left Lima in Peru after performing the Where We Are concert there. Louis is filming, and laughs as he says, "So here we are, leaving Peru. Joint lit. Happy days!"

"What do you think about that kind of content?" he asks Zayn.

"Very controversial," Zayn replies.

During the journey both Louis and Zayn joke around and Louis comes out slightly worse in the video as he finds it hilarious that a police officer on a motorbike is escorting them and they're smoking what appears to be weed— "One nil b***h! Look at this b***h! He's having a look. He's thinking, 'I'm sure I can smell an illegal substance in there.' And he's hit the nail on the head."

Directioners were very shocked when they saw the video and Liam attempted to apologize for Louis and Zayn's actions, tweeting, "I love my boys and maybe things have gone a little sideways, I apologize for that. We are only in our 20s and we all do stupid things at this age."

He also decided to share his thoughts on an article penned by journalist Jan Moir, in which she said the trust was gone, they didn't respect their fans and spoke negatively about all the members of the group, not just Louis and Zayn. Liam told his followers: "Just read a *Daily Mail* article written by Jan Moir, some of which I totally agree with but some things you are far off your game, my friend. Thank you for your lovely words, Mrs. Moir. Sorry we let you down so fantastically, maybe next time a little research is in order.

"Like so many writers before, consistently getting things wrong, looking down their noses, thinking, they are oh so right.

"Thank you to everyone who stuck with us through this, just know that we love you guys for it and it means the world.

"Hopefully, we stand the test of time and get it right in the end. I don't take this for granted and I'm extremely grateful to be here doing this. We all have a lot of growing up to do in an extreme circumstance. I'm not making excuses but it's a fact we're gonna fall short somewhere."

Zayn never takes himself too seriously.

Above: Zayn felt privileged to meet Prince William in November 2014.

Below: Not just musicians, but writers too.

Above: Taking a well-earned break to enjoy a game of soccer at the Boca Juniors stadium in Argentina.

Below left: Zayn is constantly adding to his tattoo collection. Here he is in a tattoo parlor in Dorset.

Below right: Just one of the many examples of art Zayn has all over his body.

Left: Zayn and Perrie have been together for years and have always supported each other in their careers and in their personal lives.

Below: When Zayn turned twenty-one, Perrie got him an awesome Hulk cake.

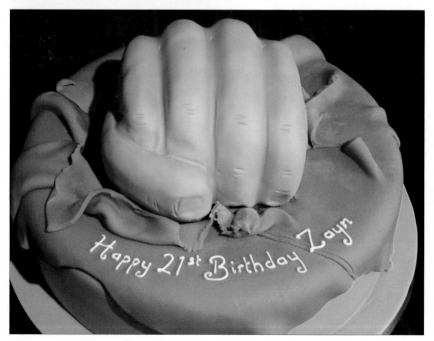

One of Zayn's final performances with 1D in Spain in December 2014.

Above: Sand artist Lee Tetzner jokes about taking a saw to his Zayn creation.

Left: Perrie Edwards was spotted shopping with Zayn's family on March 30, dispelling rumors of a split.

Right: At Madame Tussauds a tissue attendant had to be appointed after news of Zayn's departure spread.

Above: Just a few days after the shock news of Zayn's departure broke, the rest of the band appeared in South Africa, and the fans showed their support.

Left: Zayn is now working with Naughty Boy on solo material.

Right: No matter where life takes him, Zayn's family will always be there to support him.

Who knows what the future holds for Zayn?

CHAPTER THIRTEEN

FOUR

In September 2014, the 1D boys announced that they would be releasing a new album, titled *Four*, on November 17. They shared the news in a video on YouTube and to celebrate, invited fans to download a new track called "Fireproof" for free from their website. The song was written by Louis and Liam, alongside John Ryan, Jamie Scott and Julian Bunetta. Niall explained why they had chosen to give the track away to fans, simply stating, "because you have supported us so much, we wanted to give a little something back." Fans had only twenty-four hours in which to do so, and by the time the deadline was up there had been 1.1 million downloads worldwide.

The bandmates wanted to reward those who pre-ordered the album too, so for five days when fans pre-ordered the deluxe album, they received an instant download of five bonus songs. Liam explained on the YouTube video: "If you pre-order the deluxe edition of our new album before on iTunes you'll receive not three, not four, but five tracks before the album has even been released." The promotional songs were "Ready To Run," "Where Do Broken Hearts Go," "18," "Girl Almighty" and "Fool's Gold." The album quickly became Number 1 in sixty-five countries on pre-order sales alone.

Before the album was released, fans got to enjoy watching the video of "Steal My Girl." Shot in the desert outside Los Angeles, it starred Hollywood legend Danny DeVito, who was playing the part of the music video director. In the clip, fans saw Zayn dancing with two sumo wrestlers and declaring: "It's sick! It doesn't look like a One Direction video shoot, it's like some mad movie set."

Liam plays a bandleader, Louis becomes best buddies with a chimpanzee, Niall dances with an African tribe and Harry dances with some ballerinas holding umbrellas. It certainly was their craziest video to date and must have stretched their real director, Ben Winston, as there were so many people involved.

Before the video was released Winston told the *Daily Mirror*: "It's quite an exciting video. You should expect the unexpected on this one. It's weird and wonderful."

In another interview with *Digital Spy* he admitted: "I do get nervous with the videos. We've done some amazing things with One Direction, from the *This Is Us* movie to 1D

Day, to the music videos. The fans are so passionate about the boys and they care deeply about them, so I really care a lot about their opinion and hope they love everything we do."

It was actually Niall's idea to call the album *Four* because they had been together for four years and it was their fourth album. However, this time around he didn't get to write many of the songs as he had to rest after having an operation on his knee so he couldn't be in the studio with the others.

"Steal My Girl" was released worldwide on September 29, 2014, but fans in the UK had to wait until October 19. The single was leaked the day before its release, which was disappointing for the boys. It was Number 1 in Denmark and Greece, Number 3 in the UK and Ireland, Number 5 in South Africa, Number 7 in Spain, Number 8 in the Czech Republic and Number 13 in the US.

The second single the boys released from the album was "Night Changes" on November 14, 2014. Although they didn't know it at the time, this was to be Zayn's last single with the group. The video was directed by Ben Winston and saw each of the five boys taking the person watching on a dream date, only for it to end badly.

Zayn takes the girl to an Italian restaurant for a fancy meal, Liam takes her to a fun fair, Harry opts for ice skating, Louis takes her for a romantic drive and Niall has a night in with a roaring fire and board games planned. Sadly for Zayn, the girl's ex-boyfriend arrives and pours his drink and meal over his head. For Liam, the date ends when he feels sick on a ride and throws up in his date's hat! Harry attempts to do a risky ice-skating move only for them both to fall over on the ice, requiring treatment from a paramedic. Niall manages to set his sweater on fire and in the panic knocks a drink all over his date, while Louis is arrested for joking around after a policeman pulls him over in his car.

Directioners loved this video so much because it gave them a glimpse of what it would be like to date the boys in real life. The song went to Number 1 in Belgium and Indonesia, Numberin the UK, Number 11 in New Zealand and Number 13 in Ireland.

Four was a massive hit across the globe: upon release it went to Number 1 in eighteen countries. Worldwide, it sold 3.2 million copies in 2014. One Direction became the first band to have their first four albums hit the top spot in the US charts in the first week of release.

For this album, they worked with some familiar faces, but the project also brought new people to the table. Matthew Healy (from the indie rock band 1975), Scottish recording artist and songwriter Emeli Sandé and producer Naughty Boy all helped the boys pen much edgier songs than previously, but they didn't necessarily make it onto the finished album. With more than one hundred tracks, they had to whittle the choices down to their favorites.

Ed Sheeran had previously written several songs for the boys but only one track made it onto the actual album,

"18," which was a great shame. Before the release he told MTV in September 2014: "I got a call from [Simon] Cowell the other day [about the song being on the album]. But you never know, it might happen last minute where it's taken off, like that's how it works in this industry, so you never know."

American rock band Good Charlotte spent some time in the recording studio with the boys, something that Louis and Liam will never forget. Guitarist Benji Madden had tweeted back in March: "Good day today w/ @Louis_Tomlinson and @Real_Liam_Payne lotta laughs #1D #Directioners their new album is crazy. homies!! #Noice." He also shared a photo of Liam in a "Madden sandwich" (Liam in-between the two brothers) and Louis also shared with his followers: "Great working with the Good Charlotte boys today!!"

Niall had just as good a time with the McBusted boys, tweeting: "Last night I wrote a song with @Dannymcfly @dougiemcfly and @tommcfly, dougie went home, tom got peed on by his son, me and danny had curry."

The Irish band Kodaline also had a good writing session with Harry in LA, tweeting: "In the studio with @Harry_Styles in LA writing a tune, sounds massive. He's gone and done a drawing of us.. x" and they shared a picture of the drawing, too.

Naughty Boy had claimed in June of that year that the track he had written and produced with Zayn and Emeli Sandé, "One Chance To Dance," was to be the album's lead single so fans were surprised when "Steal My Girl" was released instead. They thought maybe it would be the second release but alas, it didn't even make it onto the final cut. When fans asked Naughty Boy what had happened to the track he simply tweeted: "Ask God."

In November 2014, Liam finally spilled the beans, telling *Digital Spy*: "There was a weird thing around that track . . . I just think too much was said too soon and obviously we were really stages into the album. It's a great song and I think in the end it was decided that it wasn't as much us, as much as it could be for somebody else. Zayn, who wrote the song, felt the same way about it as well, but it's a really, really good song."

The boys were immensely proud of the fact that they had cowritten ten out of the twelve tracks on the album, with Liam adding: "Now we feel like we really want to take a hold of where our career is going; to say the things we want to say, and sing about the stuff we want to sing about.

"I'd say out of all the albums we've had out so far, this is the album I've had on repeat. Whereas the other ones I haven't really listened to that much since we did them."

X Factor mentor Simon Cowell was very impressed when he heard the album for the first time, telling Capital FM: "The album's fantastic! There's probably five or six tracks I've already heard that could be singles. There's some very different kinds of songs than what we've done before, they've taken a few more risks. Most importantly, the boys love writing, they love recording.

"I went on Twitter recently to say I don't think they're going to split up, they're having too good a time! I think they could be doing this five, ten, twenty years if they wanted to!"

The tweet Simon was referring to was one he sent on August 23, 2014: "Just to clear up the rumors it is my guess and my hope One D will stay together for a very long time."

Four – Track by Track

Track 1 – "Steal My Girl' – Written by Louis, Liam, Wayne Hector, Julian Bunetta, Ed Drewett and John Ryan. Produced by Julian Bunetta, Pär Westerlund and John Ryan.

Track 2 – "Ready To Run" – Written by Louis, Liam, Jamie Scott and Julian Bunetta and John Ryan. Produced by Julian Bunetta and John Ryan.

Track 3 – "Where Do Broken Hearts Go" Written by Harry, Julian Bunetta, Ruth-Anne Cunningham, Theodore Geiger and Ali Tamposi. Produced by Julian Bunetta, Pär Westerlund and Teddy Geiger.

Track 4 – "18" – Written by Ed Sheeran and Oliver Frank. Produced by Steve Robson, Matt Rad and Sam Miller.

Track 5 – "Girl Almighty" – Written by Julian Bunetta, John Ryan and S. "Pages" Mehner. Produced by Julian Bunetta, John Ryan and Alex Oriet.

Track 6 – "Fool's Gold" – Written by Zayn, Niall, Harry, Louis, Liam, Jamie Scott and Maureen McDonald. Produced by Matt Rad, Jamie Scott and Sam Miller.

Track 7 – "Night Changes" – Written by Zayn, Niall,

Harry, Louis, Liam, Jamie Scott, Julian Bunetta and John Ryan. Produced by Julian Bunetta and John Ryan.

Track 8 – "No Control" – Written by Louis, Liam, Ruth-Anne Cunningham, Jamie Scott, Julian Bunetta and John Ryan. Produced by Julian Bunetta, Ian Franzino, John Ryan and Afterhrs Music.

Track 9 – "Fireproof" – Written by Louis, Liam, Jamie Scott, Julian Bunetta and John Ryan. Produced by Julian Bunetta, John Ryan and Ben Chang.

Track 10 – "Spaces" – Written by Louis, Liam, Jamie Scott, Julian Bunetta and John Ryan. Produced by Jamie Scott, Julian Bunetta and John Ryan.

Track 11 – "Stockholm Syndrome" – Written by Harry, Julian Bunetta, John Ryan and Johan Carlsson. Produced by Julian Bunetta and John Ryan.

Track 12 – "Clouds" – Written by Zayn, Louis, Liam, Jamie Scott, Julian Bunetta and John Ryan. Produced by Julian Bunetta and John Ryan.

Deluxe Edition:

Track 13 – "Change Your Ticket" – Written by Zayn, Liam, Louis, Niall, Harry, Sam Martin, Julian Bunetta and John Ryan. Produced by Julian Bunetta and Afterhrs Music.

Track 14 – "Illusion" – Written by Liam, Jamie Scott, Julian Bunetta and John Ryan. Produced by Julian Bunetta and John Ryan.

Track 15 – "Once in a Lifetime" – Written by Jamie Scott, Julian Bunetta and John Ryan. Produced by Julian Bunetta and John Ryan.

Track 16 – "Act My Age" – Written by Jamie Scott, Julian Bunetta and John Ryan. Produced by Julian Bunetta and John Ryan.

WHAT THE REVIEWERS THOUGHT:

Four did divide critics, with some claiming it was too similar to their previous albums and others feeling it had a much more grownup sound. *The Daily Telegraph* critic Neil McCormick gave it four out of five stars, writing in his review: "Everything is played full tilt. Songs occasionally start with acoustic guitars and dreamy restraint, but before you can say bopalula, drums are pounding out, power chords are ringing and the boys are ripping their shirts open to tell you just how much they love you baby.

"Lyrically, One Direction songs basically fall into two camps: romantic declaration and romantic longing, although it can be hard to tell them apart because they are all delivered with the same brash confidence. They are incredibly catchy, packed to the rafters with hooks and harmonies and choruses built to be sung by stadium crowds."

Jon Dolan from *Rolling Stone* gave the album three out of five stars: "There are moments on *Four* where the Big D and their cowriters let a little droll irony creep into the mix. The album's brightest song is a slick, body-moving R&B ditty called 'Stockholm Syndrome,' with lyrics cowritten by Styles about being under his girl's thumb that could also be read as a meek cry for help from deep within the prison of celebrity (even if it totally isn't). But the band mainly shows growth through the music. *Four*'s tune for the ages is "Fireproof," a subtle, pleading soft-rock lullaby any boy band, man band or unicorn band would be proud to call its own. Riding a spare bass line à la the Mac's 'Gypsy,' the guys take turns big-upping your lifesaving power over not much more than some Christine McVie-style keyboards, California guitar gold and their own billowing background vocals."

It was named one of *The Huffington Post*'s favorite albums of 2014, with critic Jessica Goodman declaring, "2014 will forever be known as the year that we realized One Direction was actually, dare we say, good. Teenagers and middle-age music critics blast "Fireproof" on the subway without shame. Stevie Nicks told us 'Steal My Girl' was one of her favorite new tracks and we can't disagree. *Four* has exactly what you want from a boy band—nay!—any band. Catchy choruses, dancy guitars and man buns (so many the man buns) make *Four* a complex, feel-good trip down young love lane."

WHAT THE FANS THOUGHT:

Can any video match up to the craziness of *Steal My Girl*? 1D superfans Elliot, Lex and Madison don't think so. They say, "Listening to the song on the album is great, but watching the video makes it even better. The concept of the video is so good, and it's nice that each of the boys have their own section, from Zayn with his sumo wrestlers to Harry with his ballerinas. It's hard to choose our favorite part of the video but we love seeing Louis sat with the chimpanzee and the ending because there's so much going on. It looks like it was so much fun to make."

Eight-year-old Brogan and Elizabeth agree: "We challenge anyone to watch the video and not smile, it's such a feel-good video. The only downside is that you're so busy watching what's going on that you don't think about the lyrics and what the boys are singing about. For this reason we'd give it four out of five stars."

As a huge Zayn fan it's no wonder superfan Imogen loves the *Night Changes* video, as Zayn looks particularly handsome in it. She says: "The song is my favorite, not only from the *Four* album but from all the albums that the boys have done so far. Watching it makes me wish I was on a date with the boys—it's so exciting to see how different their dates are. Even without the video it would still be an amazing song because it's got a good beat to it. I love the fact that they all have their own part in the song and the music video is very funny because Louis gets arrested at the end."

"Night Changes" is actually Harry and Liam's favorite song from the album. Louis prefers "Fireproof," while Zayn and Niall believe "Where Do Broken Hearts Go" is the best. Directioners couldn't wait to see their favorite songs from the album being performed on stage. The On The Road Again Tour was due to start on February 7, 2015 in Sydney, Australia, and would end eighty shows later, on October 31, 2015 in Sheffield, England.

However, when it was time to promote the album in the US and around the world, Zayn fell ill. He hadn't been seen publicly since the controversial video of himself and Louis in Peru had been leaked to the press and many Directioners were worried about him.

A few days after the others flew into Orlando, Florida, Zayn arrived, feeling much better. He'd missed an appearance on *The Today Show* and the album launch, but Harry, Liam, Louis and Niall had done a great job promoting the album, even without him there. He hadn't liked it when he found out that *Today Show* host Matt Lauer had asked the other boys: "Is it something more serious than just a minor illness? There have been rumors of substance abuse, what's going on?" but Liam had staunchly defended him, saying, "No, he's just got a stomach bug. He's okay, he's just at home. He just needs to rest.

"We're not sure yet when he's rejoining us. We're just waiting for a phone call from him."

But Zayn admitted to *The Sun* afterwards: "I'm really angry and upset by what was said on *The Today Show*. I was really ill at the weekend, that's why I couldn't fly to America.

"As soon as I'm feeling better, I'm going to join the guys and carry on with the promotion for the album.

"I was gutted to have to miss album release day but I'm going to be back as soon as I can."

Zayn's first appearance with the rest of the boys was on the *Jimmy Kimmel Show* in Hollywood but he didn't say much and he didn't look at all comfortable. When host Kimmel asked the boys who was the "most likely to disappear for a couple of days without contacting the others," they all turned to look at Zayn, who simply nodded and laughed.

And Zayn was almost certainly still not feeling a hundred percent but brightened up as the interview progressed. Kimmel asked him if he was engaged, and he nodded, saying, "I am, that's correct." Niall revealed that he was looking forward to the stag party: "I just can't wait for the stag do, it's going to be great. We're arranging it."

At the end of the interview, Kimmel asked if he could take a selfie of the boys in front of a "candy land" background but once they all got into position he declared it wasn't cute enough. He told his assistant to keep bringing various props, animals and children to them in order to make the selfie cuter. The props included cuddly toys, hats, tiaras (Zayn didn't actually put his on), his nephew (who looks like a mini Harry Styles), two twins dressed as ballerinas, a baby dressed as a cherry, a unicorn (pony), two kittens in a teacup and perhaps the world's cutest dog, Boo. Liam was holding the teacup with the two kittens inside but he was really concerned that they were getting scared. Once the photo had been taken, one tried to escape by climbing onto his shoulder so Zayn had to come to the rescue and take it from him.

In December 2014, *Now* magazine released an interview with Zayn, in which he explained why he never talks much during group interviews: "Speaking and singing are two completely separate things! I can sing and not be fazed by it, then the minute I have to speak, my brain fails me!"

Talking to fans Zayn doesn't have a problem with, which he proved on December 9, when he met thirty-six seriously ill children at a special event organized by the Rays of Sunshine charity. There, he spent time answering questions and hugging as many of the fans as he could. He joined with the others to sing "Happy Birthday" to one girl, Ellie-Leigh, who was about to turn sixteen just a few days later, and gave all the children goody bags so they'd never forget their special day. The goody bags included a T-shirt signed by Zayn and the rest of the boys, two tickets to the On The Road Again Tour and a bottle of the boys' perfume, You & I.

When Zayn looks back on his time as a member of One Direction he'll remember events like this and the difference he made. He has always kept a special place in his heart for his fans.

CHAPTER FOURTEEN

SAYING GOODBYE

2015 was to be a huge year for Zayn, although he may not have known how much his life was going to change at the start of the year. In January he got to enjoy some family time before he had to say goodbye and jet off to Australia, where the tour was starting in February.

The boys were unable to attend that year's BRIT Awards on February 25 to pick up the Best Video award for "You & I," which was a shame. It was their fifth BRIT award and they'd been up against some stiff competition from the likes of Calvin Harris – "Summer"; Ed Sheeran – "Thinking Out Loud"; Mark Ronson – "Uptown Funk" featuring Bruno Mars; and Sam Smith – "Stay With Me"; as well as five other acts who hadn't made it to the final Twitter vote-off.

Simon Cowell accepted the award on their behalf, telling the audience at the O2 in London, "Hello, this is so exciting. Sam [referring to Sam Smith], you can't win everything tonight! The boys are in Japan, and they kind of made up this speech in case they did win, and they wanted to first of all say hello to everybody, they want to thank their fans for voting because they do have the best fans in the world, they want to thank Ben Winston and Fulwell73 for making the video. I'm incredibly excited and want to officially say thank you to the boys for being just amazing. It's a great video, I'm absolutely thrilled, thank you everyone for voting."

As mentioned above, the boys were to play eighty dates on their tour in total, but Zayn performed in just sixteen shows, his last one being the March 18 show at the AsiaWorld-Arena, Hong Kong. During his final performance Zayn got very emotional, which was hardly surprising as he knew he would be saying goodbye to the boys and it would be the last time he would perform with them. Fans in the audience noticed him crying, but had no idea he was about to quit the band.

Set list:
"Clouds"
"Steal My Girl"
"Little Black Dress"
"Where Do Broken Hearts Go?"
"Midnight Memories"
"Kiss You"

"Stockholm Syndrome"

"Ready To Run"

"Strong"

"Better Than Words"

"Don't Forget Where You Belong"

"Little Things"

"Night Changes"

"Alive"

"Diana"

"One Thing"

"What Makes You Beautiful"

"Through The Dark"

"Girl Almighty"

Encore:

"Story Of My Life"

"You & I"

"Little White Lies"

"Best Song Ever"

With every tour that Zayn did with the other boys he struggled being away from his family. They tried to visit as much as they could but it was difficult, especially with his little sister Safaa still being in school. It did help that Harry, Niall, Liam and Louis were going through the same thing, but no amount of Skyping could make up for the fact that he was missing out on so much back home. Being apart from Perrie was extremely difficult and it meant they couldn't have a normal relationship. Back in March 2013, Zayn had confessed to the *Daily Star*:

"I would have cracked up and gone home by now. There's defo no way I could have done this as a solo artist.

"The lads keep me grounded and it's good to know you're not the only person going through everything."

When photos were published in March 2015 showing Zayn with his arm around a girl at an all-night party in Phuket, Thailand, the world went mad. The media claimed that he had cheated on Perrie, and a second photo was also published, which appeared to show him and the mystery girl with their hands and arms linked outside the club. Zayn was understandably upset at the allegations and tweeted on March 18: "I'm 22 years old . . . I love a girl named Perrie Edwards. And there's a lot of jealous f**** in this world I'm sorry for what it looks like x."

In fact, he was so upset by what was being written about him that he couldn't continue with the tour. In a statement a spokesperson for the band said, "Zayn has been signed off with stress and is flying back to the UK to recuperate.

"The band wish him well and will continue with their performances in Manila and Jakarta."

Of course, Lauren, the girl with whom Zayn had been accused of cheating on Perrie was upset too, as her face was splashed over newspapers and magazines worldwide, as well as on the Internet. Photographers camped outside her parents' home and her family were forced to defend her in the press.

Her mom told *The Sun*: "She was just on holiday in Thailand, posing for a snap.

"It's not as if she's a teenybopper following them around. She's more into Florence + The Machine."

Meanwhile, one of her friends hit back at Internet trolls who had threatened to stab her, telling the *Daily Mail*: "I think it's disgusting what everyone's writing about her on-line. I don't think it's her fault—I think it's blown out of proportion.

"I think she's just an ordinary girl—the fans giving her grief would have done exactly the same as her if they were in the same position. They would have wanted pics with Zayn as well.

"People shouldn't be calling her things on Twitter or Instagram or whatever. It's totally out of order. I'm not sure how Lauren's doing—I haven't really spoken to her much."

After Zayn flew back to London, the press followed his every move. He arrived back on the Friday, March 20, and Perrie was seen leaving their home with a few bags. As usual the press jumped to the wrong conclusion but her engagement ring was still on and she was standing by her man, despite what journalists might have said in their re-ports. Directioners were still getting used to the idea that Zayn wouldn't be performing with the others for a while when he announced that he had officially left the band on Wednesday, March 25, 2015.

In a statement, Zayn said: "My life with One Direction has been more than I could ever have imagined. But, after five years, I feel like it is now the right time for me to leave the band. I'd like to apologize to the fans if I've let anyone down, but I have to do what feels right in my heart. I am leaving because I want to be a normal twenty-two-year-old who is able to relax and have some private time out of the spotlight. I know I have four friends for life in Louis, Liam, Harry and Niall. I know they will continue to be the best band in the world."

The remaining bandmates also released a statement, saying: "We're really sad to see Zayn go, but we totally respect his decision and send him all our love for the future. The past five years have been beyond amazing, we've gone through so much together, so we will always be friends. The four of us will now continue. We're looking forward to recording the new album and seeing all the fans on the next stage of the world tour."

Simon Cowell added: "I would like to say thank you to Zayn for everything he has done for One Direction. Since I first met Zayn in 2010, I have grown very, very fond—and immensely proud—of him. I have seen him grow in confidence and I am truly sorry to see him leave. As for One Direction, fans can rest assured that Niall, Liam, Harry and Louis are hugely excited about the future of the band."

Meanwhile, a small minority of Directioners blamed Perrie for the split, calling her the "Yoko Ono" of One Direction (in reference to Beatle John Lennon's second wife). Zayn had said that she supported his decision to leave the group, which was something some Directioners struggled to accept.

As well as releasing a statement, Zayn also gave an interview to *The Sun* on March 27. He confessed: "I feel like I've let the fans down but I can't do this anymore. It is crazy and wild and a bit mad.

"But at the same time I've never felt more in control in my life. And I feel like I'm doing what's right—right by myself and right by the boys, so I feel good.

"You know, I did try to do something that I wasn't happy doing for a while, for the sake of maybe other people's happiness.

"And that was mainly the fans. I only ever tried to do it for the fans, and it was only ever for them."

He added that the rumors that there were rifts between members of the band were false and this was backed up by the reactions of his former bandmates in the aftermath, on-stage and on Twitter.

Harry cried during their concert in Jakarta, Indonesia, that night, and Louis had put his arm around an imaginary Zayn. In the hours that followed, Harry tweeted: "All the love as always. H" and Liam tweeted: "So glad to be in bed after a long and strange 24 hours." Liam's message really annoyed some 1D fans as they felt that he should have mentioned Zayn leaving in the tweet. They hadn't appreciated a photo Liam had shared a few days before either: it had showed the boys at a press call holding up a poster, with Liam covering Zayn's face with his hand. But Liam hadn't meant to upset anyone and had tweeted "#makinglightofasituation sorry for the laughs guys" but he had offended some fans, who at the time thought Zayn had just temporarily left the group be-cause of stress but later discovered he was gone for good.

Niall's first tweets after the news broke of Zayn leaving were: "Been a mad few days and your support has been incredible as per usual ! This in turn Spurs us on to make the best music we possibly can"; "Put on great shows / tours for you guys. You are the best fans in the world and you deserve nothing less from us!"; and "The lads and I arrived in South Africa this morning. We cannot wait to see all you SA fans for the first time and have great shows."

Meanwhile, Louis tweeted: "Been a crazy couple of days but know that we are going to work harder than ever to deliver the best album we've ever made for you guys!" and "Your support has been incredible, truly incredible, so thank you so much!"

The remaining members of 1D released a second statement to the *Daily Mail*, saying: "We're really sad to see Zayn go, but we totally respect his decision and send him all our love for the future.

"The past five years have been beyond amazing, we've gone through so much together, so we will always be friends.

"The four of us will now continue. We're looking forward to recording the new album and seeing all the fans on the next stage of the world tour."

While they were in Dubai for their last concert before a short break, Louis told *The Sun*: "All four of us are one hundred percent committed to staying in 1D."

Liam added: "It's been a tough few weeks, probably the toughest since the band was formed, five years ago. We're gutted that Zayn chose to leave, but now after a few performances as a four-piece, we're feeling confident and are determined to carry on stronger than ever."

Harry wanted to focus on the future, saying, "It's very exciting to be working on our fifth album . . . It shows how incredible the fans have been. A huge thank you to them for everything they've done for us. All the love to them."

Zayn's departure was big news everywhere and news outlets were desperate to get an exclusive. *Rolling Stone* magazine decided to print quotes from an interview they'd done with them in 2012, which up until that point had never been shared. In the interview Zayn was asked if he "expected his life to be how it is now" and he had replied: "No, not at all. This isn't what I thought I was going to be doing. I just went for the experience.

"I never went with a master plan, thinking, 'I want to be famous.' I literally went for an experience thing on the show and just hoped that . . . I guess I just got lucky."

He was also asked if he could ever go back to a normal life again and he admitted that he would like to work in the background as a producer or songwriter.

Directioners didn't really find Zayn's answers that revealing as he had never been one to hide how nervous he got in interviews and he'd freely admitted he didn't like being famous in many past interviews.

Newspapers and magazines across the world printed photos of Zayn and Perrie looking at a potential new home on the day he officially left the band, and even Zayn's mom was hounded, with the press printing photos of her enjoying a shopping trip with Perrie and Zayn's sisters. Many believed that it wouldn't be long before Zayn and Perrie set a date for their wedding because there was no longer anything stopping them—aside from Perrie's Little Mix commitments, of course. She wasn't going to be leaving her group anytime soon, which was something that grated on some 1D fans.

Zayn might have said in his statement that he wanted to be a "normal twenty-two-year-old who is able to relax and have some private time out of the spotlight" but that didn't mean he would never set foot in a recording studio ever again. In fact, he was photographed at a studio with producer Naughty Boy the day after his announcement. In the photographs that circulated afterwards, Zayn looked exhausted as he chatted to his friend. The reactions of some fans and the press to these photos was extreme and so Naughty Boy decided to set the record straight about what had happened that day. He told *Heat* magazine: "I've been his friend. He needs one. Just because we were seen at my studio, you don't necessarily just make music.

"People seem to forget that he's under so much stress, which is why he left the tour. There's a lot going on.

"People get caught up—what he has done is normal . . . sometimes being normal is to try and sort things out with your fiancée or hang around with a friend. That is normal."

However, he admitted that he would be working on solo material with Zayn at some point in the future and added: "I can honestly say Simon Cowell has been the most understanding."

Many fans were saddened to hear that Zayn was even thinking of going solo because they felt this made a mockery of his statement—they wanted to know why he said he wanted a normal life if he was going to continue to be a recording artist. They wouldn't have minded if he'd waited a few months or a year but to jump straight into a solo career, that seemed a bit heartless. Naughty Boy made the situation worse when he tweeted a link to his and Zayn's track "I Won't Mind" on SoundCloud, with the message, "Let the music do the talking guys. thank us later x" and "There is nothing but love for what was left behind. thats [sic] why we don't mind. ;) #2016 #zaughty #zindabad." He also retweeted a video, suggesting he saved Zauyghty's life and Zauyghty will rise (Zauyghty is a hybrid name for himself and Zayn).

Meanwhile, Louis could see how much the tweets were upsetting Directioners, who were already finding it hard to cope with Zayn leaving the group so he decided to fight back via Twitter: "Wow @NaughtyBoyMusic you're so inconsiderate pal, seriously how f***ing old are you ? Grow up ! #masterofallwisdom."

To which Naughty Boy replied: "@Louis_Tomlinson calm down. was talkin bout Louis Walsh cuz he didn't let someone through on X factor. Look @ the date of the tweet. #2014."

But Louis fired back: "@NaughtyBoyMusic I was talking about the video you tweeted. Clearly trying to wind the fans up ! Well you succeeded anyway. Fair play."

He told his followers, "Always have struggled to bite my tongue."

But Naughty Boy seemed keen to rile Louis up further by tweeting: "Eh? @NaughtyBoyMusic being told to grow up by wannabe football club owner @Louis_Tomlinson ??"

This time Louis didn't bother with a response.

There was a question over whether "I Won't Mind" was a new track or whether it had been written for 1D's *Four* album and not made the final cut. The *Irish Mirror* tweeted: "Zayn Malik's solo song with Naughty Boy is a One Direction REJECT tune—didn't make their album," but Louis responded with: "@IrishMirror is that an April fool?"

A day after posting the track, Naughty Boy deleted it but didn't say why. He had received hundreds of abusive messages from unhappy Directioners, so maybe this was the reason, but perhaps it was that he didn't have permission to share the material without approval from Simon Cowell and Syco? He tweeted: "no one is against anyone here. the fans made all of us. not just a chosen few. the love is alive. hate just doesn't belong there."

Zayn remained pretty silent for a while, but that didn't stop other people from sharing their pearls of wisdom. Former Westlife singer Brian McFadden reflected on what it had been like for him when he decided to leave his own band in March 2004, telling the *Daily Star*: "I haven't spoken to Zayn. I have spoken to some of the other boys but I don't really know what's going on.

"It's difficult to adapt to life on your own when you've spent so much time in a band, you kind of become a family.

"For Westlife, we became brothers and I think that was the hardest thing for me.

"Not waking up in the morning and sharing my day with four other lads, that'll be difficult for him."

Morgan Spurlock, who directed One Direction's *This Is Us* movie, told TMZ: "I think they'll stay together for a little bit longer and I think at some point Harry will probably leave."

Zayn made his first public appearance since leaving the band at the Asian Awards on April 17, in London, with his mom by his side. He was sporting a new look as he'd shaved his head, and happily signed autographs for fans before making his way inside. On the red carpet he refused to answer any journalists' questions, but that was to be expected.

He was there to collect the award for Outstanding Contribution to Music from Naughty Boy and in his acceptance speech he told the audience: "I'm not really a guy of many words, normally. I don't normally do the speeches. I'd like to thank my mum and dad and I'd also like to take this moment to thank four of the best guys that I ever met whilst being in the band and doing all the amazing things that I did. Some of the things that we did will stay with me for the rest of my life and I'm thankful for that."

Zayn will certainly never forget the crazy times he'd shared with Harry, Liam, Louis and Niall, the huge ups and downs they had as the world's biggest boy band. He'll always remember their performance at New York's Radio City Hall in 2012 because the audience members watching them were so loud. When they were leaving the venue, fans surrounded their tour van and their security team had to try and move the girls back before they could drive off.

Directioners were going crazy, banging on the windows and jumping on the back bumper of the van. The boys headed to a bowling alley to have some fun together and even managed to break the lane machinery when they threw three bowling balls down a single lane.

Also, Zayn got the opportunity to meet some amazing people through being in One Direction and he has made some lifelong friends. He met First Lady Michelle Obama and her daughters, Sasha and Malia; also, U2, Will Smith, David Beckham, Johnny Depp, Charlize Theron, Angelina Jolie and Brad Pitt—virtually every big star on the planet. One of the first famous actresses he met was Emma Watson because 1D were invited to a *Harry Potter* premiere during their time on *The X Factor*.

But he did have some regrets, too: in the early days with the group he'd been invited to Johnny Depp's studio but he refused to go because he was really nervous and didn't want to embarrass himself in front of one of his heroes. Harry, Liam, Louis and Niall went without him and had a blast, performing some songs for Depp's daughter, Lily-Rose. Zayn confessed afterward to *The Sun*: "Hopefully, there will be a next time. The boys said he was totally cool. I kind of regret it for sure and the lads said I was a scaredy cat.

"Some of our fans get so excited or nervous when they meet us and that's how I was at the thought of being with Johnny. But instead of lapping it up and enjoying it, I ran the other way."

Zayn ended his speech at the Asian Awards by saying, "Here's to the future." He was excited about what the future held for himself, both musically and personally. There was marriage to Perrie to look forward to and perhaps even starting a family. He was going to be able to see his mom, dad and sisters more and to try new things, too but he would be forever grateful to 1D and the fans who had supported him when he was in the band and hoped his fans would continue to support him as he began this new chapter in his life.

One of his new projects could involve acting, as Gurinder Chadha, director of *Bend It Like Beckham: The Musical*, told 3am at the Asian Awards that she had had a meeting with Zayn to discuss the possibility of him acting in the new musical, which was set to hit London's West End in May 2015, although she hadn't got an exact role in mind for him. She said: "We've met and spoken. He trained as an actor first, then became part of the band so I think what he'll be doing is staying true to his heart—and that's all you can ever do."

On April 20, Zayn tweeted a message for the first time in a month, saying, "Wanna say thanks to everyone that's been there for me over the last few weeks, love you all.. you know who you are x."

"The x is a kiss by the way ha it's not a mystery . . . sorry to any confused . . ."

Up until that point he had only retweeted two photos from the Asian Awards, one of himself with Indian actor Shah Rukh Khan, another where Naughty Boy joined them.

In April 2015, physicist Stephen Hawking came up with a unique take, when asked about the cosmological effect of Zayn's departure from 1D, saying: "It would not be beyond the realms of possibility that somewhere outside of our own universe lies another different universe—and in that universe, Zayn is still in One Direction."

CHAPTER FIFTEEN

WHAT THE FANS THOUGHT

Seventeen-year-old Michelle is from Hesselt, Belgium. Her dad drove her all the way to Germany with her friend Axana so she could meet the 1D boys at a signing for *Up All Night* in September 2012. It was a day that started with disappointment but ended in triumph. She had been devastated when they'd arrived only to discover that they were over eight hundred girls there so there was no chance of getting a wristband. Her dad could see she was upset so told her to search for other Belgian girls who were at the front of the line and try to wait with them. Michelle did as he suggested and picks up the story here: "Axana and I started walking then there were a lot of girls screaming and running. We thought One Direction had arrived, so we also started running where the other girls were. Suddenly we were into the barriers and we were with the first one hundred people. The people who were camping there—so the first people who were there—were just trampled; we were crushed into a sea of screaming girls. We might have been near the front, but we had to stand for twelve more hours before we would meet the boys. It was really tough, a lot of girls were crying."

Michelle and Axana received their wristbands at 3:30 and then met the boys just after 5:00. When they saw them on the stage it was "pure magic." Michelle describes what happened: "When I arrived at Zayn, he spontaneously gave me a high-five! WOW! Then I said: 'Hi, Harry!' and Harry gave me a high-five! OW, YEAHHH! Next was Louis: 'Hi, Louis!' High-five! BAM! Liam was the same, he gave me a high-five! WHOOOHOOO! Then there was our cute Irish Mullingar boy. I asked, 'Niall, can I hug you?' Niall stood up, we almost hugged, but then our magical moment was over, because Paul [Higgins, the boys' tour manager] said: 'No hug, just high-fives.' So I gave a quick high-five to the love of my life.

"Even though that day was years ago, I remember it all so clearly. It's so sad that they won't be performing as a five-piece any more. I was just scrolling on Facebook when I read the statement about Zayn quitting. I was in shock but it didn't come as a big surprise, it had just been announced that he was leaving the tour, so I saw it coming, really.

"If I'm honest, I think it's a bit egoistic for Zayn to leave in the middle of a tour. Okay, he can skip two or three concerts to rest, but he just leaves. People who bought tickets to their concerts expected to see their five idols, not four! I wish he'd have just finished this tour and then left.

"Despite this, I hated reading some of the abusive messages that people left on Belgian news sites, underneath their reports about Zayn leaving. They were so horrible and said they couldn't wait for the band to completely finish. I'm so glad this isn't going to happen for a long time. Harry, Louis, Liam and Niall are so dedicated and I can't wait to listen to their new music when they release it."

Fifteen-year-old Livia from São Paulo, Brazil, was so shocked when she found out that Zayn had left the band. A huge Directioner, her favorite songs are "Moments," "Half A Heart" and "Don't Forget Where You Belong."

She was having a history lesson in school when her friend told her that she'd read in a magazine that Zayn was quitting the band: "I didn't believe her at first, I thought the magazine was telling lies, but when my teacher left the room, I checked Facebook and a Brazilian fan site—only when I read the statements Zayn and the boys made did I believe that it was true. I started crying straightaway, I couldn't help myself. I had to rush to the bathroom. I wasn't unique in feeling this way—lots of Brazilian Directioners felt the same.

"It took weeks for the news to properly sink in. I just couldn't get my head around it. Zayn was so unique, he could never be replaced. He is such a sweet and calm person; he always knew how to make us laugh and smile. Any future One Direction songs will miss his powerful voice and his ability to hit the high notes. I honestly think One Direction without him is not One Direction but I will support them no matter and I will support Zayn if he decides to release solo material in the future. I hope that one day we get the opportunity to see One Direction whole again, even if it's just for one performance."

Eighteen-year-old Camila from Santana de Parnaíba, Brazil was equally devastated. Her favorite three songs are: "They Don't Know About Us," "Spaces" and "What Makes You Beautiful." She explained: "I arrived home from university and I saw 1D had tweeted something in their band account, I opened the link and there it was: the message from Zayn, explaining that he was leaving One Direction. At first I didn't believe [it], I was shocked. After reading it for the second time, I cried. I felt very bad, felt very empty. I didn't want to believe it was real, but it happened and I didn't want to listen to any One Direction songs for a while. It took me about two to three weeks to listen to a 1D song again. Now I see it a bit different, I understand his side and I accept it.

"The reaction to the news has been huge in Brazil. People talk about it every day. There are different thoughts on everything, but most Directioners feel the same as me. Hearts have been broken, there's been tears, people have got a bit frustrated and some still don't accept it but we will continue to support them, no matter what. In my opinion, Zayn was the best singer in the group and the next album will be very different without Zayn. His voice will be missed.

"I am very excited about the boys' next album. I loved to see the way Louis, Liam, Niall and Harry vowed to keep on working to make us happy, how they're excited for their future and how happy they are to work on the next album. I am very excited to see how everything will come out. And yes, of course, my support for Zayn will never diminish. He's still supertalented and the world deserves to hear more from him."

Fourteen-year-old Maria from the Canary Islands, Spain, was crushed when she found out that One Direction was no longer going to be a five-piece band. Her favorite three songs are: "They Don't Know About Us," "Right Now" and "Don't Forget Where You Belong." She had been campaigning for a long time for 1D to visit the Canary Islands and to find out that Zayn would never visit as part of 1D came as a huge blow to her and her fellow Canary Island Directioners: "We mourned together. It was hard to think we'd never see Zayn on stage with the others, performing in concerts, seeing him smile as part of the group. We'd miss his high notes . . . it was all so sad.

"We decided to focus on the future. We're so excited that Louis, Liam, Niall and Harry are working on new songs, a new album, and we know it will be a success. We won't forget Zayn and will always support him. We will continue to campaign for 1D to visit us and would value any support from Directioners in other countries. Please tweet #CanaryIslandsNeed1DTour, if you can."

Seventeen-year-old Gráinne from Tuam, County Galway, Ireland, was sitting on a small nine-seater minibus in the middle of Belfast city, learning about the history of the city, when she found out Zayn had left. Her favorite three songs are "Moments," "Half A Heart" and "Act My Age." She explained: "My mother called me and I answered, not expecting the words 'Zayn is leaving One Direction' to travel through the phone. She told me ever so calmly and my only reaction was to deny it, deny he was leaving us, deny he was sick of the world of fame, deny, deny, deny.

"Zayn didn't, in my opinion, get enough recognition for his beautiful voice and the loveable qualities which he brought to One Direction. For a boy that is breathtakingly beautiful you'd expect the media to be hyped about every little thing he ever did yet instead it was constant negative media, whenever they took the time to be interested in him and his personal life. I think Zayn brought a unique image and voice to the band that was like their 'glue.' He may have not been as appreciated as the rest by some, but he was the piece of the jigsaw which you needed in order to finish off perfectly.

"I've never been not excited about new One Direction songs and I don't believe I ever will be, but the thought of an album cover with four members on the front, four names thanking their friends, family and fans—well, that surely hurts a lot. No high notes that pierce your heart at first listen, that is going to truly affect us all, but of course I am excited for a new album, who wouldn't be? Zayn may release solo material in the future and no matter what, I will always support him. I fell in love with five boys, five years ago, not just four so without doubt, I will forever love and respect Zayn. I may be disappointed, heartbroken and even a little angry about Zayn leaving One Direction but I will always support the boy who, in many ways, changed my life forever."

When twenty-year-old Sarah from New York, heard that Zayn had left the band she couldn't believe it. Sarah had met One Direction with her cousin Eva back in May 2012 when they were on their Up All Night Tour. She can still remember that day like it was yesterday, saying: "We had Ultimate VIP tickets, so we had to get to [the] Beacon Theater by four in order to be able to get the seats. While waiting in line, we made friends with the people around us and still keep in touch today! As it got closer and closer for us to go in the VIP, host Stix was walking up and down the line and was asking us how we were. He noticed that I had a broken hand and signed my cast! Then we were ushered into the theater and were sat in the second row for soundcheck! After the boys finished singing, they went into the audience and started answering fan questions. One of the questions was 'What was the best gift you have ever received from a fan?' I had drawn a picture of each of the boys and planned on giving it to them when I took my picture with them later on, but Zayn was right at the end of my row so I got his attention and said, 'This picture! Say this picture!' He then proceeded to tell me that my drawing was 'Very good!' and I passed it down the aisle to him and he kept it! After fan questions my cousin and I lined up to take our picture. We were very calm up until this moment. As we got closer and closer to the boys, we got more and more nervous.

"My cousin went first to take her picture and then came my turn. I hugged Niall, Louis, and Harry and said hi, but when I got to Liam and Zayn, they both called me babe and I melted inside. Zayn calling me babe was the BEST thing to ever happen to me because he was always my favorite.

"Finding out that he was leaving was so hard to hear. Zayn brought a lot to the band. One Direction will absolutely never be the same without him. They will never be able to perform a handful of their old songs because Zayn hits high notes in some songs that hadn't even been discovered until he recorded them. I think the boys will do just fine without him, but I just hope they can carry what Zayn did for them without him.

"When Naughty Boy released demo after demo just after Zayn left it made lots of fans in the US and worldwide angry and made many feel like Zayn had been lying to fans. Some have stuck with him and some have decided not to anymore. I have found myself torn.

"If Zayn comes out with solo music, will I buy it? Will I want to? Yes. Will I? I'm honestly not sure. I am very disappointed in Zayn at the current moment in time. I feel like he lied to us about why he quit the band. He said he wanted to be a normal twenty-two-year-old but it's honestly not possible to be a normal twenty-two-year-old if you hang out with music producers, recording songs with them and dating an extremely famous girl in a world-famous girl group after just quitting the biggest boy band in the world since The Beatles. He may not have quit to go solo, but he sure didn't quit to be a normal twenty-two-year-old. He attended an awards show last week. I feel deeply betrayed by what he did to the fandom and honestly take it on a personal level. Do I think the music he has made with Naughty Boy is good? Hell, yes! Did I listen to it more than one-and-a-half times? No, because every time I hear his voice a little piece of me dies because he hurt me that bad. If he had said he was leaving to go solo I could come to terms with it. I still love him to death, but for now I just need some space between us as I come to terms with him leaving the band."

Thirteen-year-old Courtney from Cheshire, UK, has been a Directioner ever since the boys appeared on *The X Factor*. Her favorite three songs are "One Thing," "Midnight Memories" and "Story Of My Life." She was actually reading a book on One Direction when she found out he had left: "I was so shocked. Zayn's my favorite and I really thought Harry would have gone first. I was really upset— One Direction just won't be the same without him.

"The press really hounded Zayn and always wrote so many negative stories about him when he was in the band so once he left, they were even worse. They were camped outside his house and I felt really sorry for Zayn and Perrie. I'm definitely going to support him in the future because of what he did for us in his years with One Direction. I won't give up on him."

Thirteen-year-old Jadyn from Kentucky has been a Directioner ever since she first heard "What Makes You Beautiful" on the radio for the first time. Her favorite three songs are "No Control," "Act My Age" and "Little Things." Although Louis is her favorite member of the group, she was still devastated when she learned that Zayn was leaving.

Jadyn confesses: "I don't hate Zayn. I'll still love him forever but I just have so many questions I wish I could ask him. I'd love to really know why he left the group and why his fiancée Perrie Edwards hasn't quit her band, Little Mix, to be with him.

"I will support Zayn through his solo career and I am still a Directioner till the very end, I'll just always miss him. I'll always remember all the memories of the five of them together, the video diaries, the energy juice, Vas Happening . . . so many good times!"

Sixteen-year-old Nikki from Staten Island was at the boys' *Today Show* appearance, back in March 2012, and managed to meet Niall's family. She explained: "We ended up very close to the stage and right next to the barrier across from where the boys exited and entered. After soundcheck we were all talking and a man in VIP asked my friend Erin who her favorite was. She showed him her sign, which said 'Niall, I'm 100% Irish' and said, 'Niall, of course!' He laughed and replied, 'Oh, my nephew!' Then he pointed to the woman beside him and said, 'This is his mom.'

"We were all a little shocked with everything, you can say. I looked at the woman and realized she took a picture of my sign earlier. She took a few more pictures of our friends and our signs and then we talked to them. My friend Erin began talking to them about Ireland.

"I made a complete fool out of myself, dropping my sign a few times and asking Maura—Niall's mom—if she knew Zayn's mom. Out of all the questions I could have asked her, I asked if she knew Zayn's mom! I guess it was because I wasn't thinking clearly. But the whole time Niall's family were very nice. You could tell they were very proud of Niall. Then the boys came out and performed and after that we said our goodbyes and left.

"Three years might have passed since then but I still remember it as if it was yesterday. When I think of Zayn up on stage performing with the others it's hard to think that next time I'll see One Direction perform live, he won't be there.

"When the news broke, so many people came up to me in school and told me that they heard Zayn has left, but I just brushed it off. Once school ended and I was finally able to look at my phone, I received a text message from my friend, which had a screenshot of One Direction's Facebook post announcing Zayn's departure attached to it. I was in utter shock, and in front of my friends, which meant I couldn't cry. The minute I arrived home, I began to sob. I couldn't hold it in anymore. I was sad—that is the only word to describe how I felt. The same night, news of Zayn's departure was on E! News and all over the web. Some people on social media, and in person as well, began making racist and horrid jokes about the reason Zayn left, which was really upsetting. The majority of fans in the US focused on how 1D would be losing his talent and wondering what he might bring out in the future. Zayn leaving was such big news everywhere, everyone was talking about it. My grandma even called me to tell me!

"What did Zayn bring to One Direction? Well, he has a very unique voice. He can go low and then high in a second. He always hit his notes and even added his own flair to the songs live. You always saw his passion while he sang. Although the others are able to cover his solos and notes, no one can do it like Zayn. The uniqueness of his voice is something no one can replace. Zayn did not carry the boys, but expanded their range, voice-wise. I will miss all that Zayn brought to the group. I will miss seeing him perform next to the other four boys, and I will miss seeing him frequently due to being in the band, press-wise.

"Despite Zayn leaving the group, I plan on sticking with the boys and supporting them until they decide to call it quits. I am very excited and anxious to hear the next album. I want to see what direction they plan to take without Zayn, whether it be the same type of music or something completely different. If Zayn decides to go solo, I may be upset with his choices but I will support him, no matter what. I did not fall in love with the music, I fell in love with those in it. Due to this, I will support each one of them for as long as I am able to."

CHAPTER SIXTEEN

STANDING ON HIS OWN TWO FEET

Zayn might have spent a lot of time in the studio with Naughty Boy during his first few weeks away from One Direction but their friendship didn't last long. Zayn was furious when a demo he had made with rapper Mic Righteous was leaked in June 2015. He hadn't wanted anyone to hear their cover of Rae Sremmurd's "No Type" and decided to show how he felt via twitter. He tweeted: "@NaughtyBoyMusic you fat joke stop pretending we're friends no one knows you," and "Someone learned how to upload a video . . . maybe now he should learn how to use logic ha you ain't s*** but a faker."

Naughty Boy had tweeted at the time of the leak: "[T]hat had nothing to do with me or Zayn, something was stolen from the hard drive that had nothing to do with the rapper involved."

However, rapper Mic Righteous did end up taking the blame, writing on Facebook: "Zayn wants the tune out, he ask me to be on the song, shah (naughtyboy) told me that his label wont let him release any music for the next two yrs.. So you know what i did? I did it for him, for you. And at the end of the day they cant say no to me, i work for the people not the industry."

Zayn clearly wasn't happy with either Naughty Boy or Mic Righteous and decided not to work with them again. He also decided to make big changes in his personal life, ending his engagement to Perrie only a few weeks before they were due to move into their new house together. Instead of packing up his belongings in his London bachelor pad he was going to be staying put, for the time being at least. Zayn hadn't put it on the market and it had sentimental value, it was the first home he'd ever owned. He loved its modern design and the fact that he'd built his own pub/shed in the garden so he could relax without worrying about the paparazzi. When they first split, the media reported that he'd ended things with Perrie over text but Zayn soon set the record straight, telling Fader: "I love her [Perrie] a lot, and I always will, and I would never end our relationship [of] over four years like that.

"She knows that, I know that, and the public should know as well.

"I don't want to explain why or what I did, I just want the public to know I didn't do that." Zayn was spotted out and about with a couple of different girls in the next few months and even posted a selfie of himself topless with an unknown woman in the September. His first official girlfriend after Perrie was American model Gigi Hadid and she would appear in the video for his first solo single "PILLOWTALK." They were spotted out on dates together in November 2015 and their relationship was confirmed in February 2016. Zayn and Gigi had hinted that they were just friends but when Zayn was asked on Westwood One's Zach Sang and the Gang radio show whether it was cool to have his girlfriend in the *PILLOWTALK* video he replied: "Yeah, that was cool. That was something different—and yeah, we enjoyed it. It was fun. We had a lot of fun on set." In a separate interview with *LOVE* magazine, Gigi confessed: "We cope with the trolls by having each other. "It's the same thing as dating someone within the industry rather than out of the industry. You only understand it when you're literally experiencing it."

Zayn had wanted his solo album to be the best it could be so he wanted to work with an amazing producer. He decided not to work with the producers behind any of One Direction's hits. The man he chose was Grammy Award winner Malay Ho, who had previously worked with the likes of Alicia Keyes, John Legend and Frank Ocean.

Malay was a producer that Zayn had admired from afar so he initially asked his people to get in touch to see if Malay would be interested in working with him. He was thrilled when Malay agreed to a meeting and they soon hit it off. Malay was very impressed with Zayn's strong songwriting skills and his vocal range. He was blown away when he heard him sing "PILLOWTALK" and "fOoL fOr YoU" for the first time and was keen to get recording straight away.

Although they spent some time making the album in a recording studio they also recorded in the luxurious Studio Suite at the Palms Casino resort in Las Vegas, in a hotel room in Beverly Hills and in some woods with a mobile studio. The time Zayn spent recording with Malay was lots of fun and not as structured a s his recording sessions with One Direction had been. Zayn was very much in control and was able to make the type of music he'd always dreamed about.

Malay confessed to EW.com: "I think it felt liberating for him to be able to really portray his voice the way that felt natural for him." During the interview he also revealed how certain tracks came about. They had written/recorded most of "BeFoUr" in Zayn's hotel room in Las Vegas after a night partying at the swanky Drai's Beachclub and Nightclub while rapper Big Sean performed. Malay explained: "We were sitting backstage in a VIP area and [Malik] was just telling me, 'It's crazy being here in Vegas. I've literally been all over the world with One Direction. I've done this before, but not like this. Not by myself, not this way, not here with the intention of working on my own music.' I was like, 'Wait a minute— I've done this before, but not like this—that's a song, man.'"

When fans got to hear the album for the first time, many were impressed with "INTERMISSION: fLoWer" a track Zayn sings in Urdu, his dad's native language. Zayn sings about how [translated from Urdu] "Until the flower of love has not blossomed, this heart will not be in peace. Give your heart to me." It was a song that came straight from Zayn's heart and didn't need to be worked on, the first time he recorded it, it was perfect.

Zayn released his first single "PILLOWTALK" on January 29, 2016. It was a huge hit worldwide, topping the charts in sixty countries and Zayn became the only UK artist to debut at Number 1 in the US. Fans had expected it to be more adult in nature than a typical One Direction track after he'd told the *Sunday Times* prior to its release that he'd written it about sex, "so pure, so dirty and raw."

Two more versions were later released, an acoustic version and a remix with rapper Lil Wayne. Both critics and fans were impressed with Zayn's first solo offering. Lewis Corner from Digital Spy gave the single four out of five stars and wrote in his review: "The final result is more Justin Timberlake than Robbie Williams. There's a sophistication that will keep young fans listening, while pulling in a new, more style-conscious audience. And that's on both sides of the Atlantic, and everywhere else inbetween."

The *Irish Times* named it their track of the week and said: "It's Zayn's first solo track and it's a grownup affair. It's all about making *lurrrrve*, and features expletives—it's a firm step out from 1D's MO. Which was to be expected. The twist is the sound—think nouveau R&B (like Miguel) with a blogwave backing. It's slick, and the accompanying video is suitably abstract."

Zayn superfan Ffion from Cheshire might only be eleven but she loved the single and the video. She says: "It's so good that Zayn's finally been given the musical freedom to do the kind of music he wants to do. He's really expressing himself in this song. I might be younger than his target audience but I can still appreciate how talented he is, both as a songwriter and as a singer. I'm not surprised the single was a big hit around the world, I couldn't get it out of my head for weeks."

Both with "PILLOWTALK" and with his debut solo album, Zayn wanted his fans to see the real him, he wanted it to be a hundred percent authentic. He didn't want to rush getting the album out, but at the same time he didn't want to keep his fans waiting too long. He decided to release his second single, "Like I Would" on March 10 and then release his album on March 25.

"Like I Would" reached Number 30 in the UK charts and Number 55 in the US. Critics were impressed, with *The FADER* magazine reviewer describing it as an "euphoric, super danceable breakup jam."

Releasing his album on the one-year anniversary of the day he left the band seemed like the perfect time to Zayn. For many fans it was nice to have something to look forward to on that day as the year before many fans hadn't been sure that he'd be releasing any more music as he'd said in his statement: "I am leaving because I want to be a normal twenty-two-year-old who is able to relax and have some private time out of the spotlight."

Mind of Mine might have topped the charts worldwide as soon as it was released but Zayn still had a lot of promoting to do. He had numerous big TV interviews and magazine interviews plus special performances . . . and he was keen to continue working on his second solo album. He didn't want to sit still for a minute!

In an interview he gave to *NME* (*New Musical Express*) just days before Mind of Mine was released, Zayn admitted how he'd felt when he decided it was time to leave One Direction in 2015: "I called my security and I was like: I need to sort out a plane, I want to go home. I don't know how I knew, but I just did. So I chatted with my cousin. Listened to a few songs. Just . . . waited for my plane to come."

A year after leaving One Direction, Zayn admitted that he wasn't really close to any of the boys apart from Liam, and that they only chat on the phone; they hadn't met up in person yet, despite the fact that they both live in London.

In interviews Zayn doesn't like to dwell on the past or his former band members and much prefers talking about his new music. He thought *Mind of Mine* was the perfect title for his debut album because "it's really reflective of the whole experience that I want to give the listener. I wanted it to be almost like a brainstorm. It's just music and it's just whatever you're feeling at that moment in time."

In an interview with *The FADER* before its release he confided: "Once they [the fans] hear it, I feel like they will understand me a little bit more. For ten years, this album has been in my brain, and it's just been there, sat with me, needing to be out."

Zayn wanted his new music to be very authentic and show the real him. As well as releasing his album on the March 25 he also released the video for his second single, "BeFoUr." He shot the video in the Miles Platting district of Manchester and it wasn't at all glamorous. It showed typical "Northern lads" having fun, "It wasn't like, 'I'm still Jenny from the block,' " he confessed to *NME*. "It was more like: this is what I used to do. Go down the chip shop, hang out with my boys in the car park. We never set fire to cars, but . . . I seemed to find myself in situations that weren't necessarily the best situations. Getting wound up by stuff people said."

Mind of Mine topped the charts, making Zayn's dream of being a successful solo artist come true. It debuted at Number 1 on the *Billboard* 200 albums chart in the US, making Zayn the first male solo artist from the UK to have his first album debut on top! When he left One Direction he had no idea whether people would accept him and his solo music—he knew lots of One Direction fans may never forgive him for leaving the band and other people might never take him seriously as an artist, but he needn't have worried. He was simply too talented to not top the charts!

Mind of Mine Track List:

Track 1: "MiNd Of MiNdd" (Intro)
Track 2: "PILLOWTALK
Track 3: "iT's YoU"
Track 4: "BeFoUr"

Track 5: "sHe"

Track 6: "dRuNk"

Track 7: "INTERMISSION: fLoWer"

Track 8: "rEaR vIeW"

Track 9: "wRoNg"

Track 10: "fOoL fOr YoU"

Track 11: "BoRdErZ"

Track 12: "tRuTh"

Track 13: "lUcOzAdE"

Track 14: "TiO"Deluxe Edition

Track 15: "BLUE"

Track 16: "BRIGHT"

Track 17: "Like I Would"

Track 18: "She Don't Love Me"

Fans were thrilled, both with the album and with the *BeFoUr* video. Superfan Maria from California tweeted: "After a year of heartbreak Zayn has released his own album. An album with just his voice. I'm crying happy tears."

Her thoughts were echoed by fans all around the world with Ziyad tweeting: "A year ago he made the whole world cry and now he made them proud. Thank you Zayn."

Fifteen-year-old Gaby from Saltillo, Mexico initially found it strange listening to Zayn singing on his own. She said: "I was so used to hearing him sing with the other boys that it took a while to get used to him being a solo artist. He is so talented, it's so good to hear his high notes again. If I had to choose one track from the album to be my favorite, I'd have to go for 'iT's YoU,' but it's really hard to just pick one. He's so sincere on this album and so real."

Twenty-year-old Taylor from Knoxville, Tennessee thought the whole album was great. "I can't stop listening to it. My favorite tracks have to be 'Like I Would,' 'TiO,' 'dRuNk,' 'BeFoUr,' and 'PILLOWTALK.' 'Like I Would' is easy to dance to and I love the way his voice moves up and down. 'TiO' is so different to what I was expecting and that it made it even better. 'dRuNk' is simply pleasing to sit and listen to . . . and he sounds amazing. 'BeFoUr' is not like the rest of the album with the way Zayn sounds so it really stands out. My absolute favorite has to be 'PILLOWTALK' because it was the first song we heard from the album and it set up such a great expectation that did not let down."

Eleven-year-old Rachael from Cheshire agrees: "They're my favorite songs from the album too. I was never really into One Direction but I heard 'PILLOWTALK' on the radio and I was eager to hear more. I think Zayn has an incredible voice and I can't wait to hear his second album!"

Music critics were equally as complimentary. Glenn Gamboa from Newsday.com wrote in his review: "*Mind of Mine* now positions Malik at the tail end of The Weeknd's promotional cycle and before Frank Ocean unleashes his much-anticipated follow-up to *Channel Orange*. Malik's brand of R&B bridges the gap between the two, with a bit of pop-leaning Justin Timberlake thrown in for good measure.

"The mix is obviously right on time, considering how his first single 'Pillowtalk' debuted at Number 1, something One Direction has never done. "Pillowtalk" is a good introduction to the album, featuring the push-and-pull of a relationship that refers to their bed as 'It's our paradise and it's our war zone.'

"However, *Mind of Mine* only gets deeper and more impressive from there . . . whether it's the decadent, lush 'Drunk' or the stark 'Wrong,' warmed up nicely by Kehlani, *Mind of Mine* is clearly Malik's creation, one that may take him to unexpected new heights just by being himself."

A reviewer from the *Boston Herald* thinks that the album shows that Zayn is a better singer than Justin Bieber, adding: "This is an ambitious, mature, modern R&B 14-song collection, filled with songs about love, lust and longing. It certainly doesn't cater to the 1D audience. It's also very good. 'iT's YoU' is a slow, atmospheric, strings-laden gem. Zayn's expressive voice hits the highest of falsetto notes and is as smooth as satin sheets. It's destined to became a slow-dance favorite. By contrast, 'TiO (Take it Off),' an uptempo soul-stirring jam, will get lots of plays in clubs just before last call. It's bold and sexy, unlike the quiet, pleading tunes that comprise most of the album."

What can we expect from Zayn's second solo album? We'll have to stay tuned! All we know is that he wants to make it even bigger and better than *Mind of Mine*, and he's determined to keep making great albums for a long time to come.

ABOUT THE AUTHOR

Sarah Oliver has written numerous books about celebrities, including *Inside Taylor Nation: True Encounters with Taylor Swift*. She is also the author of *Around the World with One Direction*, *One Direction A-Z*, and *Robert Pattinson A-Z*. She appeared in the documentary *One Direction: All for One*. She lives in Widnes, United Kingdom. Lesser Gods will publish Sarah's biography of Miley Cyrus in 2017.

Ed Sheeran A+

The Unauthorized Biography

David Nolan

ONE

SO Hebden Bridge

"I remember big hills," Ed Sheeran says when recalling his West Yorkshire childhood. "I know I lived at the top of one."

The area of West Yorkshire where Ed Sheeran is from is known as Calderdale. Tucked to the east of the Pennines, Calderdale is very proud of the young man born there on February 17th, 1991. The local paper likes to refer to Sheeran as the "Calderdale Singer-Songwriter."

If Calderdale were a song type it would be a mash-up. It's a series of contrasts that sit side by side: the tea shop and the tower block; the brass band and boutique hotel; the Mosque and the Mecca Bingo Hall. It's independent and likes to wear its independence proudly on its collective sleeve. But there's one part of Calderdale that doesn't just display its independence—it screams it from the rooftops. It's the part of Calderdale where Ed Sheeran began his life: Hebden Bridge.

As you drive into Hebden Bridge from nearby Halifax, a roadside sign states that the town lays claim to "500 Years of Creativity." As you drive out, the reverse sign tells you that you are leaving by camply proclaiming: "That was *so* Hebden Bridge."

It is home to artists, hippies, TV producers and seekers of alternative lifestyles. It's also the "most lesbian" town in Britain, with more same-sex female couples than anywhere else. But Hebden Bridge is very aware of its image and reputation and isn't averse to sending itself up now and again—there's even a furnishings shop called "Home...Oh!"

The groups of creative and alternative incomers that descended on the area in the 1970s saved a declining mill town and turned it into their own little slice of Bohemia. Hebden Bridge is Bohemian simply because the people who moved there decided they wanted it to be that way. The creative enclave is a base for many people working in

Manchester, Leeds and Halifax because of its central location and handy train links. The charming late nineteenth-century train station that serves the town obviously made an impression on the young Ed: "I remember being four and wanting to be a train driver—that was the only thing that interested me," he told KidsofGrime TV. Not that he's entirely given up on the idea: "I'll become a train driver one day."

Ed's parents, London-born John Sheeran and Imogen Lock, could be said to fit the Hebden Bridge profile pretty well. Both are passionate about the arts: John as an art lecturer and curator, Imogen as a promoter of the arts through her work as a PR consultant to the creative industries. "His mum was very much into PR," says Gordon Burns, Ed's cousin. Burns is a radio and TV presenter, best known as the face of *The Krypton Factor*. "His dad used to run these art galleries—he's very deep into the arts—John Sheeran's a nice, easygoing guy. All the Sheerans are like that, incredibly laid back. That comes all the way down through the family—easygoing, fun and gentle—and Ed seems to have it as well. Nothing fazes him, his feet are firmly on the ground, he knows what he's doing. Which is what I'd expect of a Sheeran."

Imogen Sheeran's creativity would also come out through her love of making jewelery. Today, her handmade items are proudly sold at Hebden Bridge's Earth Spirit shop on Market Street. The shop's owner Catrina Gledhill is keen to highlight Ed's local connection, especially as the jewelery designs are intrinsically linked to Ed's childhood: "Ed grew up in Hebden Bridge so it's great that Ed's talented mum, Imogen, has chosen to supply a local business," she told the *Hebden Bridge Times*. "Many of the items from the collection are based on his favorite sweets, such as Liquorice Allsorts and Smarties, or on Ed's song lyrics."

The Sheerans loved the town so much they didn't let the fact that their work regularly took them to London and Manchester put them off living there. For John, it was as curator of the Dulwich Picture Gallery in southeast London. For Imogen it was as a media consultant for the National Portrait Gallery in the capital and then, nearer to home, working for Manchester Galleries just over the Pennines.

Their first son Matthew was born in 1989. Perhaps aware of the changes their lives would undergo after starting a family, John and Imogen left their jobs and set up an arts consultancy business together in 1990. Ed—known when he was young as Teddy—was born a year later. They still went where the work took them, usually London. Most weekends would be spent traveling to and from the capital with their two young sons in tow. The Sheerans would play music in the car to while away the time on the long journeys. "Basically, my parents had to commute and I'd go with them," Ed later explained to *Q* magazine. "It'd be the same albums over and over again—Dylan's *The Times They Are A-Changin'*, Clapton's *Unplugged*, Joni Mitchell's *Blue*. Now, listening back to all that stuff, it just reminds me of homely, warm stuff. It's really cool."

The trips were so regular—and the album choices so consistent—that Ed began to learn the words and eventually he started to sing along. The albums on the Sheerans' car stereo may have spanned a thirty-year period, from 1964 (Bob Dylan) to 1992 (Clapton's *Unplugged*), but they all clearly share a gentle, acoustic vibe that would make a clear impression on Ed, as would the more traditional aspects of Irish folk music: "The first album that introduced me to music was Van Morrison's *Irish Heartbeat* with Irish traditional group The Chieftans," he later told *OnStage*. "The first music I heard was trad music. That was a major influence. There was an Irish folk band called Planxty that I was brought up on."

John Sheeran's musical tastes seemed to dominate and his acoustic and traditional choices would prove to have a lasting effect on Ed. But anything overly rock 'n' roll was frowned upon in the Sheeran household. "My dad's never been into rock music—ever," Ed told *The Age* newspaper in Australia in 2012. "We've never had a Queen CD in the house."

Motown seems to have been as up-tempo as things got chez Sheeran and Stevie Wonder—who Ed would perform with in 2012 at the Queen's Diamond Jubilee Concert—was a particular favorite: "My dad had [Wonder's 1974 album] *Fulfillingness' First Finale* on record," Ed later told *The Guardian*. "That was the first Stevie album I heard and there was a track called 'They Won't Go When I Go', and that's been one of my favorite songs ever since. He's just great."

Music producer Jake Gosling, who worked with Ed on his early EPs and later the + album, believes that Sheeran's upbringing was key to his later life as a musician: "He's from a very creative background, his mum and dad have supported him all the way," he later wrote on his blog. "He was brought up surrounded by artists, painting, sculpture and the obscure. For any growing mind this set a light. Ed uses his music to communicate what he really feels and speaks from the heart."

The creative, musical atmosphere within the family clearly had an effect on both boys: Ed's brother Matthew would go on to study music at university and is now an award-winning classical composer, having received a young composer's award at the annual Presteigne Festival in 2010 and a composition award at the international Shipley Arts Festival the same year. Ed and Matthew look like twins—both have the flaming red Sheeran hair and both share the same sharp facial features.

As a young child, Ed's features would cause him issues, some of them continuing into his teens. He had what he would later describe as a "massive" birthmark on his face removed by undergoing laser surgery. He would later claim that having the birthmark led to him developing a speech impediment. "When I was younger I had a really bad stutter and had to do a lot of speech therapy," he revealed to *The Sun* in 2011. "I overcame it when I was about thirteen or fourteen years old. I still have a bit of a stutter when I get excited but it's not as bad as it was."

The birthmark and the stutter—plus poor eyesight and hearing, not to mention his distinctive shock of red hair—seemed to have weighed heavily on the youngster. He would later describe his childhood as "slightly depressing." But it's hard to imagine a child being more nurtured and encouraged than he was. His was a deeply creative family environment—Ed would say an early ambition of his was to "sort of paint and stuff"—and he even sent some of his early paintings into BBC kids' show *Blue Peter*.

Vacations for the Sheerans usually meant traveling to Ireland, where their family roots were strong. Ed's grandparents Bill and Ann had moved from London to County Wexford. Their marriage in the 1950s had caused a scandal in the family: Bill was a Protestant, Ann a Catholic. Ed would go and stay with his grandparents at their farm for the summer alongside other young members of his extended Irish family. Idyllic. His grandparents' farm was a playground for him and his young relatives. After a day spent running around collecting chickens' eggs, Ed would take a sleeping bag and camp out in the huge barn with his cousins—the Sheeran farm is still a retreat for Ed to this day. "Ann, Ed's grandma, is gentle and laidback," Gordon Burns told me. "Bill, his granddad, was a leading light in the British Boxing Board of Control and used to be an amateur boxer. Bill is an easygoing, laidback guy."

The Irish connection also provided an upbringing steeped in the love and appreciation of music. In terms of his own involvement, Ed would join his mother singing in a choir at a very young age, the starting point for his love of song: "It's just a love of mine that's been embedded into me since I was young—it was constant," he later explained to the OTUmusic website.

To be nearer their work—and as it became time for Ed to start school—the Sheerans moved south to the beautiful Suffolk market town of Framlingham. By way of contrast to the groovy, hippy vibe of Hebden Bridge, Framlingham is steeped in history that makes the Calderdale town look like a newcomer. Dominated by its 12th-century castle, the town can trace its roots back to the *Doomsday Book*. Framlingham guards its history and beauty closely with a conservation area at the heart of the town designed to protect its charm. With a population of less than 3,000 it is as tasteful and well-appointed as anywhere in Britain and the town and its surrounding areas are very proud of Ed Sheeran—the local newspaper likes to refer to him as the "Framlingham Singer-Songwriter." Obviously. "Growing up in Suffolk—because it's the countryside—it was very free and easy and relaxed," was how Ed would later describe his new home.

Ed was enrolled into the Sir Robert Hitcham Primary School on College Road in Framlingham. The school describes itself as providing a "happy and caring Christian learning environment, where individuality is celebrated, achievement nurtured, and every child empowered to reach their highest spiritual, educational, and personal potential." It's the oldest elementary school in Framlingham and is named after the former owner of Framlingham Castle.

John and Imogen Sheeran continued with their art consultancy, but having creatively-minded parents wasn't always appreciated by young Ed. "I remember during the yoyo craze my mum wouldn't spend £8 and made me one out of jam jar lids and string. Can you imagine taking that to school? But now I see it was cool and I realise how amazing my parents are for not giving me that stuff—all the kids I knew with everything aren't really in a good place right now."

Ed's love of singing was augmented by a gift from an uncle that was a little more eagerly received than his jam-jar-lid yoyo—a guitar. Ed would later become fascinated by the instrument after seeing Eric Clapton play at The Queen's Golden Jubilee concert in February 2002. Clapton's performance also convinced Ed that he should concentrate on acoustic guitar: "I used to be really into guitar-driven music," Ed later told *Total Guitar* magazine, "Guns N' Roses songs and stuff like that. I saw Clapton play 'Layla' at the Golden Jubilee. That song is wicked." Ed watched the event on television—Tom Jones, Sir Elton John and Sir Paul McCartney played as well. Ten years later, Ed Sheeran would play alongside them at the Queen's Diamond Jubilee concert.

There were a few guitar lessons to set him on the right path, but Ed mainly did it his way, taking a view that he seems to have stuck with: if a thing's worth doing, it's worth doing properly...and doing yourself. "When I started playing guitar

I was practicing seven hours a day, just going through it," he would later explain to OTUmusic. "Friends would come round and say, 'Come out,' and I'd say, 'No I'm doing my music—I can't waste time.' That actually happened." A template for the future was already being set. Don't muck about. Do it properly. Work hard: "Nothing is worth having unless it comes with hard work," says Sheeran today.

He began to listen to more music from ever-widening sources. If it seems precocious to be doing this at such a young age... that's because Ed Sheeran was precocious. His youth and enthusiasm began to combine with his eclectic tastes in music, plus the continuing influence of his parents' acoustic-based Hebden Bridge record collection. Van Morrison and Joni Mitchell albums nestled next to Elton John's *Greatest Hits* album and The Beatles in the Sheerans' record collection. Plus it's hard to imagine that their Framlingham home didn't have a reasonable collection of albums by John Martyn. The Anglo-Scots folk and jazz musician, who died in 2009, was notable for his use of the Echoplex tape delay effect, which allowed him to build up loops of sound and rhythm both live and in the studio. The technology Ed Sheeran would use in years to come was different, but the effect would be remarkably similar to the sound that Martyn produced. By way of contrast to Martyn's mellifluous soundscapes, Ed also professed a liking for punk and nu-metal, perhaps as a small act of rebellion against his family's mellower tastes: "I was kind of brought up as a bit of a *Kerrang!* kid and when I was younger I loved bands like Blink 182, Offspring and Linkin Park," he later confessed to *The Guardian*.

A cousin then introduced Ed to rap. Jethro Sheeran had already worked as a model and actor and must have seemed impossibly glamorous to young Ed. In 2002 Jethro was making inroads into a career in music. He had launched himself as a rap act under the slightly more street name of Alonestar, had acquired Simon Webbe of boyband Blue as a manager and was getting ready to tour with the likes of Blazin' Squad. Before he was ten Ed Sheeran was listening to Jay-Z and Eminem. Then there was Tupac Shakur and The Notorious B.I.G. The gangster rappers were all across the news in the late 1990s after their violent deaths were attributed to rivalry between acts from the East and West coasts of America. The music and what it represented was as far removed from rural Suffolk as is possible, but the young Ed became enthralled. "You might look at Eminem and Bob Dylan and say they're two totally different acts," Ed told WatchMojo.com when asked about his diverse influences. "But all you have to do with Eminem is put a guitar behind his words and it's a very similar thing. Folk music tells stories and hip hop tells stories. There's just a beat that separates it."

In later years this hodgepodge of influences would baffle reviewers, who couldn't get a grip on Sheeran's music and its origins. He wasn't like other musicians because his frame of reference was different thanks to his age: "I was born in '91 so most of my musical growing up was done from 2000 onwards," he later explained to the *Daily Telegraph*. "If I'd been born in the 1980s most of my musical growing up would have been through the Blur and Oasis period so I would have been a hardcore indie fan."

Though still very young, Sheeran seems to have received a surprising amount of leeway from his parents in terms of how he lived his life. This was to have a dramatic effect on him and his future when he was barely eleven years old. "I've never really been a day person and I used to stay up at night and watch the music channels," he later explained to *Q* magazine. "This video came on at about four o'clock in the morning, just this dude's mouth singing and it turned out to be 'Cannonball.' "

The dude in the video was Damien Rice and seeing the "Cannonball" video in the early hours of the morning would shape Sheeran's musical trajectory and change his life. The video, a bizarre collage of seemingly random images of scribbled words, toothbrushes and cats—with occasional glimpses of Rice's mouth—may have made an impression on Sheeran, but at the time it didn't make much of a dent in the charts. It would take several re-releases and two years before it would peak at Number 19 in the UK charts.

Irish singer-songwriter Rice was not necessarily the most obvious artist to connect with an eleven-year-old boy, but there's a great deal about him that would directly inform Sheeran's later work. Rice's raw, emotional style, his confessional lyrics and stripped-down acoustic style would all feed into the Ed Sheeran we know today. Rice also possesses the ability to generate a communal live experience that appeals particularly to women—again, territory that Sheeran now occupies. The similarities continue: Rice had ploughed a defiantly independent path to get to where he was, releasing his album *O* on his own DRM label and organizing his own gigs, another pair of routes that Sheeran would take. What's more, the songs on *O* were largely inspired by Rice's relationship with Dublin-born musician Lisa Hannigan, who also sang on the album. The pair fell in love during the making of the record: "That had just kind of happened through the making of *O*," Rice later explained in a rare interview with Ireland's *Hot Press* music paper. "So the record felt like a record of creativity and love, and just that whole sense of coming together with a bunch of people—and in particular with Lisa.

We just worked really well together. I loved her taste. Whenever I'd do something and she'd comment on it, most of the time I'd just completely agree. We just were very, very compatible: in the studio, on the stage. But when that relationship changed it just made it very difficult because we never had the space from each other, to get used to the change.

Again, there would be a connection to Ed's work. Sheeran's + album would also be centered on his relationship with one person, his childhood sweetheart Alice. Rice's influence was so great that it was something Ed would rarely fail to mention in virtually every interview he did after he began to gain attention. Sheeran's highlighting of Rice and the way his music informed his own work has done a lot to send Ed's fans in the Irishman's direction.

The "Cannonball" video would stir Ed into immediate action: "The next day I went out and bought his album *O*," he later explained to journalist Tom Doyle. "I remember coming home and sitting in my room with my JVC CD player and listening to [second track] 'Volcano' over and over again. I couldn't get past that song. It was the intimacy and the way he conveyed emotions."

At the age of eleven Ed Sheeran's life had taken a dramatic turn. Music began to dominate, but what happened next would make him feel that music was something that he could not only enjoy, but that he could create himself.

IF YOU ENJOYED THIS BOOK YOU MAY ALSO LIKE:

Inside Taylor Nation: True Encounters with Taylor Swift
Sarah Oliver

Ed Sheeran A+: The Unauthorized Biography
David Nolan

Sam Smith: The Biography
Joe Allan